Manny Rubio

Scorpions

Everything About Purchase, Care,
Feeding, and Housing

Filled with Full-color Photographs
Illustrations by Michele Earle-Bridges

BARRON'S

CONTENTS

A NEW INTEREST IN SCORPIONS

An accelerated interest in ecology and biodiversity, combined with television's ability to transport us to the farthest reaches of our planet, have exposed us to a plethora of new and wonderful wildlife. Among these are the smaller and less-difficult-to-maintain forms, terrestrial arthropods. Animal importers suddenly have found a demand for an untapped resource of previously overlooked animals.

The Scorpion Surge

We are seeing a widely increasing interest in keeping and breeding scorpions since the publication of the previous edition of this book. To satisfy the call, a greater-than-ever number of pet dealers are carrying a variety of scorpions as part of their livestock. This has led to a broadening availability of previously unobtainable species.

Additionally, in the past few years, a resurgence in the scientific study of scorpions has led to the modification of some existing data and the discovery of new data, resulting in recent changes to the classification of scorpions. Molecular biology and DNA analysis are being used as advanced tools to demonstrate evolutionary affinities among many forms of plants and ani-

This tiny, pregnant Orthochirus serobiculosus negebensis *is missing its left chelae.*

mals. This change in methodology and redirection of resources has caused considerable discussion and some disagreement among scientists. Because habitat destruction and a myriad of other problematic alterations of the natural world are eliminating species before they can be described, scientists are questioning whether limited funds and time are being properly applied in making a wholesale number of changes at this time. It is little more than choosing priorities. Sadly, good old "go out in the field and turn rocks" field biology is heavily outweighed by the "pressing need" to publish in scientific journals. This "need" is easily filled with lab-based molecular biology.

To educate potential owners better about more suitable ways of caring for their animals, it is timely to update the text, add new information, and change most of the photographs. The revision is born.

People and Pets

Ever since humans began keeping pets centuries ago, there has been a fascination with the unusual—the more bizarre the better. The practice grew as travel flourished and has become more popular than ever. Since the 1940s, hundreds of thousands of American homes have been awakened every morning to the melodious song of a canary, the chirping of a colorful finch, or the raucous squawking of a parakeet. What child did not have at least one goldfish during his or her formative years?

For decades, millions of colorful freshwater and saltwater tropical fish have been imported annually from waterways throughout the world or raised in tropical fish farms. Large, magnificent parrots, cockatoos, and other parrotlike birds became so desirable and scarce that a network of smugglers founded a lucrative trade in them. Although dogs, cats, and tropical fish remain the pets of choice, inquisitive minds have become enchanted with the more exotic animals. The majority of these are plentiful in the wild, easy to collect and transport, and can be sold rather inexpensively. Care must be taken that overcollecting combined with habitat destruction does not severely reduce the numbers of these new pet species. Many conservationists see captive breeding as an effective means of limiting the impact on wild populations.

The New Pets

Keeping amphibians and reptiles (affectionately known as herps) was the first of this new trend. In the past few decades, an array of insects and spiders (mostly tarantulas) has found a solid place among pet owners. Recently, scorpions have claimed a substantial following. With the increasing availability of additional new and exciting species, interest is growing rapidly. This bias is logical; keeping smaller, exotic pets has been a basic tenet of European and Oriental animal lovers for years. These generally less costly animals have a fraction of the maintenance requirements, can be kept rather simply on a few shelves almost anywhere, and (at the very least) are equally as interesting as any other pet.

What Is a Pet?

There is some question about using the term pet. The *American Heritage Dictionary of the English Language* describes a pet as "an animal kept for amusement or companionship" or "an object of the affections." Scorpions will adapt and respond to having their needs fulfilled. They commonly become active when sensing the vibration of a cage top being opened and food being offered.

Realistically, invertebrates can be considered amusing in that their habits are extremely engaging. However, it would be a sizable stretch to assume that they offer companionship and that we can show affection toward them. If you are interested in these traits, perhaps you should look to vertebrates, most particularly warm and cuddly, highly affectionate, responsive mammals, as pets instead.

The Remarkable Scorpion

If you are searching for a remarkable animal whose unusual behavior and day-to-day actions will captivate and tempt you to spend hours just observing it and the characteristics that make it an amazingly efficient predator, I suggest you keep a scorpion. In a brief time, you will understand why these small creatures have

Hadrurus arizonensis *is an easy to maintain, active, large scorpion with a mild venom.*

survived for millions of years without undergoing major external physical changes. By applying a little imagination, you will see characteristics that have inspired the creation of many of the bizarre aliens and other creatures seen in science fiction motion pictures.

You Can Contribute

As old and as common as scorpions are, compared with other land animals, very little has been written about their natural history. In fact, only a handful of scientists are currently studying them. The toxicity of some species' venom is well documented, but practically nothing is known about the life histories of hundreds of others. This is an important consideration when contemplating acquiring and maintaining obscure species. Successful captive maintenance and breeding of arachnids is in its earliest stages, and much more must be learned. This affords an exciting opportunity for conscientious, dedicated keepers to observe and document previously unrecorded information. Likely behavioral patterns will be found that are shared by a variety of taxa, while others will be new, previously unreported discoveries.

Although emphasis has been predominantly placed on tarantulas, the two major avocational societies (American Tarantula Society and British Tarantula Society) actively solicit and print articles from serious amateur arachnologists. The Internet provides several active sites through which a great deal of information is exchanged among a wide range of interested

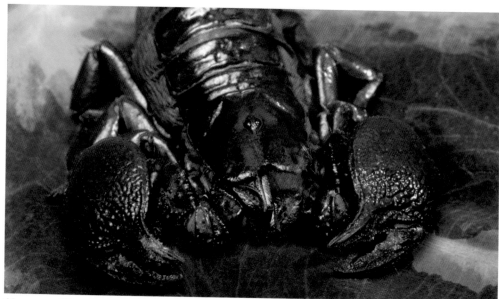

Close-up of **Pandinus cavimanius.**

scorpion keepers worldwide. It is obvious from initial contacts that there is a commonality and friendly interrelationship among the participants. The goal is to provide greater understanding of scorpions and enable others to care for them more properly.

Consider this small book to be a door into a fascinating new world. It will provide the first steps in understanding scorpions and how to maintain them and will prepare you for whatever further involvement you may choose.

A Few Things to Consider

1. One must be cautious when making generalizations about any form of animal life because exceptions always exist.

2. Very few pet shop employees, or naturalists for that matter, are knowledgeable about keeping scorpions. Pet shops with a large selection of nicely displayed and maintained tarantulas and scorpions will likely be better sources of information than those that have only a few. Asking a couple of key questions will quickly uncover whether you know more than the employees do.

3. Many scorpions do not have common names. Even if they do, these names may vary greatly from place to place. Also, different species may be known by the same common name in different regions. The scientific name not only provides the proper label for the animal but is a universally understood reference to each particular species. This makes communicating with other keepers less complicated.

4. Not all scorpions are from arid regions, and some form of moisture is very important to their survival.

5. Generally, darker scorpions live in relatively moist, forested areas, whereas the lighter-colored forms inhabit arid and grassland environments. There are numerous exceptions. Many have colorations and patterns that match the substrate of their environment.

6. The taxonomy (systematic arrangement) of scorpions is currently being revised because the classification was done at end of the nineteenth and early-twentieth centuries. Arachnologists believe hundreds of new forms are waiting to be discovered and identified.

7. Scorpion keeping is a refreshingly new area of natural history that is wide-open to observing, discovering, learning, and teaching.

8. Scorpions with very large chelae (pincers) usually have less-toxic venom and are less likely to sting. However, they are more likely to use their chelae to grab and hold on. Prey is procured by grabbing and crushing. Scorpions with very thin, long chelae usually have potent venom and are likely to sting, frequently with minimal provocation. Venom is used for procuring prey.

9. The venom of the vast majority of scorpions is not considered dangerous to humans. However, several Scorpions can cause serious envenomations. Out of the approximately 1,500 scorpion species described to date, only a small number (less than 20 percent) have been identified as being potentially dangerous to humans.

10. Venom toxicity varies greatly from taxon to taxon and among different animals within a species or from different parts of their range. Other variables are the amount of venom the scorpion recently expended on prey or predators, the number of consecutive stings to this victim, the amount injected, the mass (weight) of the victim, the person's general health, and the elapsed time prior to medical attention. The quantity of venom injected can be controlled by the scorpion, and not all stings result in the injection of venom. Care should always be taken to avoid being stung. Never underestimate the potential danger.

11. Individuals are affected differently by scorpion venom. Certain people are highly sensitive to specific chemical components of venoms and will react violently. Others may find a sting little more than a minor inconvenience.

12. The first scorpion sting may sensitize the victim to a more severe second encounter.

13. The overall length of a scorpion is measured from the anterior margin of its prosoma (head) to the tip of its straightened metasoma (tail).

14. Never forget that the life and well-being of a captive animal is your responsibility.

15. Experts do not have all the answers; they have more questions.

The large chelae of **Smerigurus vachoni** *crush small prey.*

SCORPION NATURAL HISTORY

Scorpions live in a variety of habitats—rain forests, woodlands, deserts, grasslands, and many places in between. The vast majority prefer warmer tropical or subtropical climates. However, some forms have invaded unusual areas, a few of which may be surprising.

Different Environments

The intertidal zone: In various regions of the world, a few species of small scorpions (less than 1.3 inches [35 mm] in length) live within the intertidal zone. Known as littoral scorpions, they eat the myriad tiny invertebrates that thrive within seaweed, tidal wrack, and decaying sea creatures that have washed ashore.

Tropical zones: Several species in various tropical regions of the world (for example, some *Tityus, Centruroides,* and *Chaerilus*) live within termite mounds and feed almost exclusively on termites. Because of their diminutive size, termites are opportunistically eaten by (almost any small or immature) scorpions that come upon them during periods of abundance and availability.

Mesobuthus martensii is an excellent climber and is frequently out-and-about in subdued daylight.

High elevations: A few taxa live at elevations higher than 13,000 feet (4,000 m) in the Sierra Nevada Mountains of North America and in the Himalayas of Asia, and at 18,000 feet (5,500 m) in the Andes of South America. They too are small and spend months under rocks and in burrows covered by snow and ice. Survival must be precarious. However, experiments have demonstrated that some scorpions can survive temperatures below freezing.

Intraspecies Differences

Scorpions of a given species may vary widely in size, pattern, coloration, venom toxicity, and habitat choice in different portions of their range. The influence of specific microhabitats, such as soil types and hardness, types of rock, amount of ground litter and cover, moisture gradients, seasonal temperature extremes, and prey availability all limit the distribution of

This 4th instar **Hadrurus pinteri** *is in a semi-defensive pose.*

scorpions. To survive for so many millions of years, scorpions have had to adapt and diversify.

Sand dwellers (psammophiles) have numerous setae (hairlike appendages). These setae increase the surface area of their long, slender legs and feet, permitting better footing in loose sand.

Most rock dwellers (lithophiles) are flattened and elongate with thickened, pointed setae on their body, legs, and feet. They have curved ungues on their feet to facilitate moving freely on and within rocks and crevasses. Their metasomas are long and thin, and are carried to the side rather than being elevated as in most other species.

Burrowing scorpions (fossorial) are characterized by stocky, robust body with short legs and large, powerful pedipalps and chelae.

Cave dwellers: Some scorpions (troglobites) live deep in the lightless world of caverns and caves. Because there is no need to see in the dark, the eyes of many are reduced in size and/or number or are completely absent. They usually have extremely slender, colorless bodies, legs, and pedipalps, all adaptations and results of living in cracks, under rocks, and in the recesses of caves. Scorpions adapted to living proximal to cave entrances are known as troglophiles and may or may not have reduced eyes and other characteristics of troglobites.

Arboreal scorpions are small, lithe, and extremely agile climbers. They are frequently encountered in buildings. Some climb high into trees, living within holes and cracks in the bark, while others choose the basal portions of bromeliads. Since we are at the very early stages of exploring the rain forest canopy, many new scorpion species probably await discovery there.

Each of these physical differences has a drawback. Some species are so habitat specific that they have difficulty negotiating other environments. This is an important consideration when attempting to keep these animals.

Buthacus leptochelys nitzani *rapidly digs to seek refuge under a rock.*

Adaptations for Survival

In addition to providing support, the scorpion's hard exoskeleton provides it with a rigid, protective coat that is commonly colored to match the general habitat in which it lives. This provides the scorpion with a degree of camouflage. The scorpion's flat, elongated shape enables it to squeeze into very small, tight areas. Its venom-injecting apparatus and strong pedipalps and chelae, combined with its quickness to run and react, make a scorpion a formidable, dangerous warrior and predator.

Scorpions have among the lowest metabolic rates in the animal kingdom. Add to this the great quantity of food they consume in a single meal and the energy they conserve by not moving about very much. It is easy to see why they can go a long period without feeding.

No arthropods are better at conserving water than desert scorpions. A waxy coating on the exoskeleton makes it all but impermeable to water (in both directions). Water intake of most desert scorpions is acquired from their food. Feces are passed in a nearly dry state due to a high content of nitrogen and minimal amount of water. All scorpions breathe through ventrally located spiracles, and their book lungs minimize moisture loss during respiration. Some species have flaps that cover the spiracle entrances. By seeking refuge in burrows, under rocks, and in ground litter, scorpions avoid the hottest times of the day, remain cool, and further minimize moisture loss.

Predators and Life Span

Although humans kill millions of scorpions annually, they remain a meaningful part of the food chain. Aside from cannibalism, large cen-

A 4th instar Centruroides hentzi *facing head down, secreted in a crack in a dead branch.*

tipedes, spiders, and some ants have been recorded as predators. Lizards, a few snakes, frogs and toads, birds, and mammals also take their share.

In the American West, scorpions form a large portion of the diets of grasshopper mice and burrowing and elf owls. The sand-dwelling shovel-nosed snake, *Chionactis* spp., also from the desert Southwest, is not only immune to scorpion venom but appears to feed on scorpions and centipedes almost exclusively. A few other predators are resistant to their venom. In Africa and Asia, meerkats, mongooses, and baboons systematically search ground litter to find scorpions and then break off the telsons or entire metasomas to avoid being stung before eating them.

If you have read this far, you are most likely seriously considering getting a scorpion as a pet. I suggest you spend a bit more time thinking about it.

Do You Really Want a Scorpion?

As you read, you will learn that scorpions are not pets. You can expect little or no recognition of your presence. They remain mostly secluded throughout nearly daylight hours. Nearly all their normal surface activities occur in the darkness of night. It is stressful for the animal to be uncovered and disturbed and is destructive to their carefully prepared microenvironment.

If a scorpion can avoid being poisoned or squashed, evade becoming a meal, capture enough prey, and not desiccate, drown, freeze, or cook, it has the potential to live for several years. Generally, smaller species are short-lived, perhaps two to four years being typical. Larger scorpions have been reported to live 20 years or longer. Since very little is known about the natural history of most forms, there surely

Liocheles australasiae and its diminutive 2nd instar offspring.

must be exceptions. If properly cared for, a scorpion seems to have its best chance of surviving to old age in captivity.

Being Aware of the Potential Danger

Approximately 25 scorpion species have been recorded as being lethal to humans. All but a few of the known lethal scorpions belong to the family Buthidae, but there are reports of potentially lethal forms in other families. One of these, *Hemiscorpius lepturus*, is a member of the family Hemiscorpiidae and produces highly toxic venom. A species of forest scorpion, *Heterometrus swammerdami*, is reputed to pack potent venom and be extremely aggressive. I have not been able to verify the toxicity of its venom, so the claim might be totally unfounded. This very large, reddish brown scorpion is rarely exported from its native tropical India. It belongs to the family Scorpionidae.

Heterometrus longimanus from Southeast Asia.

Of the many thousands of people who are stung worldwide each year, an estimated more than 4,000 die. As recently as 30 years ago, the number of annual fatalities was estimated to be in the tens of thousands. Although the most dangerously venomous scorpions inhabit the deserts of northern Africa, there must be relatively few incidents of stings in that area because of the comparatively small number of recorded fatalities.

Most deaths occur in the rural and urban regions of Latin America, principally parts of Mexico and Brazil. Here the culprits are a few small but highly venomous species of *Centruroides* and *Tityus* that are abundant, actively forage, and are nimble climbers. They thrive within buildings and houses where nighttime encounters with humans are frequent. Children under the age of three, the elderly, and persons that are sickly or have weakened immune systems, have hypertension, or are extremely allergic to their venom are the primary casualties. There appears to be no correlation between a

— TIP —

When Not to Keep Scorpions

Most people have a negative reaction to scorpions and respond to them with revulsion. If inducing that response is a motivating factor in keeping them, I suggest you choose some other way of "proving your machismo." Scorpions, indeed all arthropods, are viewed unfavorably by many because certain people promote these misguided reactions and dispense inaccurate information.

═══ CAUTION! ═══

An Ounce of Prevention

Avoiding a potentially hazardous situation is the smartest kind of prevention. Since very little is known about the venoms of many scorpions and people have different reactions to being envenomated, I believe that **there is no situation where a scorpion should be picked up with a bare hand**. All scorpions should be treated as though they are dangerous, and never be handled.

variety of allergies (for example, to peanuts or dust) and scorpion venom. Antivenin is rarely available or affordable in rural areas that are far away from major medical facilities.

The value of antivenin treatment for scorpion stings has initiated considerable debate among toxicologists when compared with the success of antivenin used for venomous snakebites. They universally agree, however, that primary first aid and any additional treatment deemed necessary by a qualified medical attendant is the best course of action.

In captivity, the potential hazard of serious consequences is compounded because inexperienced pet store personnel and buyers have difficulty in distinguishing potentially dangerous scorpions from the many hundreds of species that are less life threatening. In fact, several potentially dangerous African and Latin American scorpions are sold in the pet trade.

Several visits to pet shops that have a selection of scorpions nicely displayed in individual pet cages exemplified the intrinsic danger of misinformation. Mixed in among the more harmless scorpions were innocuous-looking specimens of death stalkers, *Leiurus quinquestriatus*. When the managers were told that it is one of the most dangerously venomous scorpions in the world, the specimens were usually removed from the display or labeled as such. In most cases, the pet shop managers said that the death stalkers had been purchased with a variety of other scorpions from large, commercial animal wholesalers and that the pet shop had been assured that they were all safe to handle. This problem arises because a very discerning and experienced scorpion authority is needed to identify most taxa.

Understanding Your Commitment

An owner has an obligation to maintain any captive animal properly and humanly, whether it is a dog or scorpion. The keeper must be mature enough to assume the responsibility for the animal's well-being, housing, and safety. There is the added necessity of providing escape-proof housing.

Scorpions are highly adaptable, capable of surviving under less than favorable conditions. Their ability to endure with little attention is not a reason to care for them improperly. Because they spend so much time in hiding, are not effusive or responsive (unless they are hassled), cannot be handled, and have relatively few needs, there is a tendency to neglect them. Like other animals, scorpions will dehydrate and/or starve if not properly looked after. Living things have a value and you as a keeper must be responsible for their well-being.

UNDERSTANDING SCORPIONS

To the uninitiated, a scorpion looks like a miniature lobster or crawfish. Not so! They are all invertebrates (animals without backbones) and arthropods, but that is as closely related as they get. A lobster or crawfish is a crustacean, and a scorpion is an arachnid. In fact, scorpions are much more closely related to spiders than crustaceans.

A Scorpion's Place in Nature

Although there are few examples, fossil evidence indicates that the most recent scorpion ancestors (400–425 million years ago during the middle Silurian) were aquatic—with gills and legs—and looked very much like those species living today. Some of the first scorpions to live on land (most of the time) were very small. However, at least one (*Praearcturus gigas*) was huge, approximately 3 feet (1 m) in length. Now that is one big, powerful, impressive predator!

Modern scorpions have adapted to live in a wide variety of habitats from arid deserts to moist rainforests, and from below sea level to

Advanced breeders have successfully bred colorfully patterned Hottentotta trilineatus.

high in mountains. One species has been found at an elevation over 13,800 feet (4,200 m) in the Andes Mountains. Although small in size, scorpions are an extremely important part of the food web. It is not uncommon for three or four different species to live sympatrically (in the same habitat) or in very dense communities. All scorpions are venomous and carnivorous, consuming a large number of invertebrates and occasionally very small vertebrates to help maintain a balance among the species.

Scorpion Taxonomy

Taxonomy is the science of classifying living things. As scientists learn more about a species, they frequently need to reevaluate and change its classification. Many scientists are currently working with scorpions, so the process of accu-

The Seventeen Scorpion Families

Bothriuridae	Liochelidae
Buthidae	Microcharmidae
Chactidae	Pseudochactidae
Chaerilidae	Scorpionidae
Diplocentridae	Superstitioniidae
Euscorpiidae	Troglotayosicidae
Hemiscorpiidae	Urodacidae
Heteroscorpinidae	Vaejovidae
Iuridae	

Taxonomists follow a protocol that accepts the most recently published findings (in a peer-reviewed journal) as current. This debate is well beyond the scope of this book. For this edition, I follow the findings of L. Prendini and W. C. Wheeler in their 2005 article in the journal *Cladistics*. By using a variety of physical and molecular characteristics, approximately 1,500 currently recognized species are divided into seventeen families. They are listed alphabetically in the accompanying table.

Some are further divided into subfamilies, which are in turn divided into genera, species, and in some cases, subspecies. The validity of subspecies is undergoing considerable debate among zoologists and taxonomists. Some believe that the current classification of many subspecies is poorly defined, subjective, and unwarranted.

Because many of the physical characteristics employed to differentiate taxa are very small, a dissecting microscope is needed to see them properly. Separating genera and species necessitates accurate and careful investigation and demands great patience and skill. The coloration and size of specimens of the same species vary from different microhabitats, so they cannot be used as valid distinguishing characters in most cases.

rately classifying them is evolving rather rapidly. Currently, there is a major split in the classification. Because I am not a taxonomist, I am unable to formulate a definitive opinion.

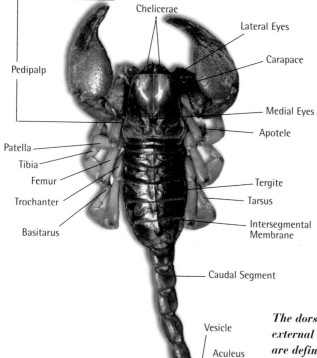

Chelicerae
Lateral Eyes
Carapace
Pedipalp
Medial Eyes
Apotele
Patella
Tibia
Femur
Tergite
Trochanter
Tarsus
Basitarus
Intersegmental Membrane
Caudal Segment
Vesicle
Aculeus
Telson

The dorsal (left) and ventral (opposite page) external characteristics of scorpions are defined in these images of **Opistophthalmus ecristatus.**

The 690-page *Catalog of the Scorpions of the World (1758-1998),* which was published in 2000, lists all the scorpions known and categorized to 1998. However, no single source is available to identify them. New forms have been described since then, and many more will be in the near future. With considerable delving and the availability of a university or museum library with expansive arachnid literature, the serious scorpiophile may be able to make valid identifications.

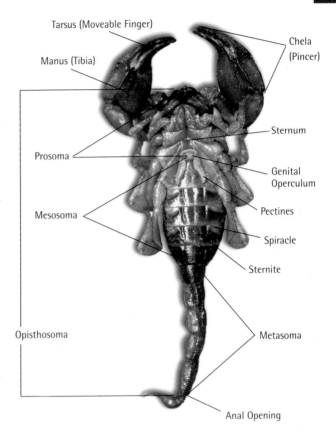

Labels: Tarsus (Moveable Finger), Manus (Tibia), Chela (Pincer), Prosoma, Sternum, Genital Operculum, Pectines, Spiracle, Sternite, Mesosoma, Opisthosoma, Metasoma, Anal Opening

Scorpion Anatomy

Most people are familiar with a scorpion's shape, and all species look very much alike. Scorpions are considered very primitive compared with most other land animals. In fact, scorpions are the most ancient arachnids found so far. They have been extremely effective in adapting, persisting on land for the estimated 325–350 million years since their ancestors emerged from the water.

All scorpions gather their body heat from external sources and are incapable of producing their own heat. In very hot environments, they are almost always nocturnal. Some temperate and rain forest forms are active during overcast days and when the canopy prevents strong sunlight from reaching the ground. Different species have different optimum temperatures in which they carry on daily life functions. A drop of 10°F (5.7°C) in nighttime temperatures and a change in seasonal temperatures of 15°–25°F (8.3°–14°C) are required by most species to

remain healthy and acclimated and to initiate a reproductive cycle. To simulate these cycles accurately, temperature variations should coincide with an adjustment in the length of light and dark periods.

A Close Look

Although it is beyond the scope of this book to discuss in detail the anatomy of scorpions, it is important to learn all the body parts and their characteristics to identify many species. The most obvious external parts are discussed here, and the others can be seen in the illustrations.

The chelicerae medial and lateral eyes of this **Babycurus jacksoni** *are clearly discernable.*

Internally, scorpions have nervous, circulatory, respiratory, reproductive, and digestive systems.

Like all arthropods, a scorpion's body is covered by a thin, waxy, rigid exoskeleton (made of chitin) that supports and protects the internal structures. It is the base for a variety of sensory receptors, spiracles (breathing openings), and other biologically significant openings to the outside of the body.

Prosoma

The body is divided into two major parts, the prosoma (cephalothorax) and the opisthosoma (abdomen). Dorsally, the prosoma is covered with the shieldlike carapace. The chelicerae are partially sheltered by the carapace and project from under its front. Chelicerae are preoral mouthparts used to tear and grind food, and they are found in all arachnids.

A pair of median eyes and smaller lateral (as many as five pairs) eyes are located on the carapace. Median eyes appear to function as very primitive viewing organs, capable of perceiving depth and spatial relationships as well as forming an unsharp visual image. They are light sensitive and appear to be used for celestial navigation and to differentiate light and dark (for example, day and night). Lateral eyes are as much as three times smaller, react more quickly to working in darkness, and may be the most light sensitive of any arthropod. They appear to be mostly responsive to the light-dark cycle and to set scorpions' biological clocks. A light-sensitive area on the metasoma has recently been discovered in several different scorpions. Its function is not yet known. Some rare, very small scorpions that live in dense forest litter and caves are eyeless.

Opisthosoma

The opisthosoma is comprised of the wide, bulky mesosoma (preabdomen) and the elongated, tail-like metasoma (postabdomen). Seven tergites (dorsal, transverse chitinous plates) combine to form the dorsal surface of the mesosoma. The flexible tissues that enable the rigid parts of the exoskeleton to articulate are called the intersegmental (pleural) membranes. The metasoma is made up of five articulating ringed segments and ends with a bulbous telson. The telson is not considered to be part of the metasoma. The needle-sharp, venom-injecting part of the telson is the aculeus (stinger). The roundish part, the vesicle, contains paired venom glands. A small pointed prominence, the subacular tubercle, is located near the aculeus on some taxa. Taxonomists use this small prominence as a primary characteristic to distinguish some forms.

It is important to note that the metasoma is not a tail per se, but a continuation of the abdomen. It contains part of the intestine, the hindgut, nerves, arteries and veins, and muscles, and it supports the telson. The metasoma is very muscular and, aside from stinging, is used for digging, scraping dirt, balance, and climbing. The anal opening is located in the soft tissue of the last (fifth) segment, where it connects with the telson.

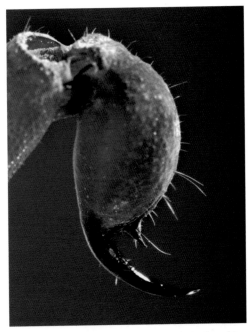

The bulbous vesicle of **Babycurus jacksoni** *shows the long, needle-sharp aculeus and smaller subacular tubercle.*

Appendages

Four pairs of jointed legs (all located on the cephalothorax) provide locomotion and are used for digging. The portion connecting each leg to the body is called the coxa and is followed (in order) by the trochanter, femur, patella, tibia, basitarus (tarsomere I), tarsus (tarsomere II), and apotele. Small ungues (lateral) and dactyl (median) clawlike appendages are attached to the apotele.

Pedipalps are analogous to arms and hands. The pair of pedipalps has six segments. Starting at the body, they are the trochanter, femur, patella, tibia, and tarsus. The last two segments are greatly modified into chelae (pincers or

The tarsus and basitarsus of **Babycurus jacksoni** *show sensory setae and claws for climbing rocks.*

sometimes massive chelae are capable of exerting remarkable pressure, cracking and mashing all but the hardest invertebrate exoskeletons.

Underside

The shapes of the parts of the ventral region of the body between the legs (coxosternum) are primary characteristics to differentiate among scorpion families. The two genital opercula (fused plates covering the genital aperture) are found on the midline just behind and posterior to the centrally located sternum. Eight small spiracles (openings) on the broad, transverse sternites (ventral chitinous plates of the mesosoma) carry air into the book lungs (respiratory organs). These spiracles are efficient in minimizing moisture loss during respiration.

Sense Organs

Although scorpions have very poor eyesight, they have an arsenal of highly responsive mechanosensory and chemosensory receptors that would make any hunter proud. While using scent, air movement, and vibrations, they sense the presence of predators, prey, mates, water, temperature, and light, as well as several other stimuli that remain undiscovered.

Pectines are a pair of unusual comblike appendages located on the ventral surface just behind the last pair of legs. Unique to scorpions, these organs are important for sensing ground vibrations and are used by males for sensing pheromones during mating. Research has shown that pectines have touch and smell receptors.

hands). The manus (a modified tibia) is the palm and fixed finger. The tarsus is the movable finger. Although most of the jointed segments are comparably named to those found on legs, pedipalps are not legs. Pedipalps are used for grabbing, holding, and crushing prey; for protection as weapons and shields; and for digging. They also carry some exceptional sensing organs.

The inner surfaces of the fixed and movable fingers of the chelae have a series of granules and pointed "teeth" that enable them to hold tightly and crush prey. Some males have conspicuous, strongly serrated "teeth" that are lacking in females, making them sexually dimorphic characters. Scorpions with larger,

Setae are hairlike projections found on many parts of the body, legs, and pedipalps, giving the scorpion a pronounced hairy appearance. Some are not visible without magnification. At least three different kinds of movable and immovable setae have been described. They are known to receive tactile, thermal, chemical, or humidity sensations. However, more research needs to be done to see if the immobile ones have a sensing function.

The most important setae are the long, thin trichobothria found only on the pedipalps. They are incredibly sensitive to air movement and airborne vibrations. They can sense the slightest movements of prey, other scorpions, or threatening situations. It is likely that some contacting the ground may pick up those vibrations as well. Trichobothria locations, numbers, and arrangement are consistent within a species and are used as taxonomic characteristics.

Tarsal (foot) setae pick up substrate vibrations and may also sense chemicals and water/humidity. Bristlecombs (clumps of setae) on tarsal and basitarsal segments increase the surface area of the "foot" (like snowshoes) and are adaptations for expediting travel on sand. Bristlecombs and tarsal setae are excellent clues to the habitat preference of a particular scorpion but are not necessarily easy to notice.

Other nearly microscopic receptors called slit sensilla are found on the legs and metasoma. When any pressure is placed onto the exoskeleton, these slits open slightly. Depending on the amount of pressure, the scorpion makes adjustments in body movements and posture. Additional slit sensilla, on the basitarsae of at least

one pair of legs, seem to sense ground vibrations, like those produced by the movements of insects. The scorpion uses the sensations received by the two opposing legs to triangulate on the prey and to determine its direction and distance.

Stridulation

Several scorpions can make sounds by stridulation—the rubbing of one part of their body against another. A few *Opistophthalmus* scorpions rub their chelicerae and cephalothorax together to produce a hissing sound. Some *Heterometrus* make a similar sound by stroking pedipalp bristles (groups of setae) with segments of their first legs. Other genera stridulate by rubbing telsons to metasomas, pectines to sternites, and pedipalps to first walking legs. *Rhopalurus junceus* stridulate loudly by movement of their pectines. *Scorpio maurus* bang their telsons on the ground, producing clicking noises. These sounds appear to be warnings to potential predators.

Pectines of a male Babycurus jacksoni.

VENOM AND ENVENOMATION

Venom is a mixture of complex chemicals (low-molecular-weight peptides) that destroy cellular components when they enter cells. More than 100 of these peptides have been identified in scorpion venom.

Venom's Function and Toxicity

The primary function of venom is to capture and subdue prey. The use of venom defensively is secondary. All but a very few extremely uncommon scorpions produce venom. Fortunately, only about two dozen species are considered potentially lethal to humans. Biochemists are involved in a great deal of research on venom, particularly on how it affects the human body and as a possible treatment for several human illnesses.

Venom toxicity varies from genus to genus, species to species, and (frequently) within a species. It also tends to be somewhat specific to scorpions inhabiting a particular area. Why? The reason is mainly because the quantity of

Smerigurus vachoni is "feisty" and quick to defend itself.

each venom component varies. Aside from inheritance, environmental conditions, the kind of prey that is most frequently encountered and eaten, or simply a normal physiological variation among specimens may be the reason for the differences.

The Sting

The stinging method used by a scorpion for envenomation is quick and efficient. The muscular metasoma is held high, telson poised, ready to deliver a rapid downward thrust enabling the needlelike aculeus to pierce the exoskeleton or skin of its target. The scorpion is apparently able to feel that a sting has been effective, because if the aculeus has not penetrated, it will continue to probe until it reaches its mark. Setae on the telson are likely important sensors. Struggling prey may be stung several times while being held in the chelae.

The aggressive feeding nature of this 3rd instar **Hottentotta frazwerneri** *is shown as it stings a cricket equal to it in size.*

The amount of venom injected can be controlled by the scorpion: greater doses for larger prey animals, less for smaller ones. In some cases, no venom is injected. This is known as a dry sting. A similar phenomenon is seen in venomous snakes. The aculeus may remain imbedded for a few seconds or simply stabbed in and then immediately withdrawn and returned to a ready position. No matter which method is employed, the scorpion's venom apparatus makes it an extremely efficient predator.

The reaction of humans to the stings of nearly all scorpions is minimal and most commonly equated to being stung by a bee or wasp. However, some scorpions cause much more severe reactions—a few are fatal. The pain and other reactions associated with scorpion envenomations can be of consequence. A sting is always a threat.

Infection or tetanus: One factor that is normally overlooked in a sting is the possibility of developing an infection or tetanus. Tetanus is a potentially fatal disease; more than 50,000 people die from it each year worldwide. Some people have allergic reactions to tetanus antiserum. The most recent immunization for tetanus, an injection of tetanus toxoid, is considered permanent. If you are uncertain of the immunization method, a tetanus booster should be administered every few years. All scorpion

Better Safe than Sorry!

Preventative measures and those actions taken while getting to a hospital after a scorpion sting can save your life.

If you think that you are likely sensitized to scorpion venom, be prepared. An allergist can prescribe a specially designed kit (EpiPen) to counteract the early stages of anaphylactic shock. An EpiPen is a small, personal, easy-to-carry, auto-injecting apparatus for administering a 0.3 mg dose of epinephrine. Epinephrine is a drug that induces the body to secrete adrenaline and combat extreme allergic reactions. It is highly effective against ant, bee, wasp, and scorpion stings. Another device, Anapen, is produced in Europe and essentially does the same thing. It is smaller, more compact, and has a finer needle point.

Although considerably less efficient, over-the-counter antihistamine medicines like Benadryl, Ephedrine, Tagamet, or Zantac are worth using if an EpiPen is not available.

are candidates for serious complications from an envenomation. The average, healthy adult usually incurs minimal reactions to an envenomation from all but the most toxic scorpions.

Usually, the body's defensive system will react to a scorpion envenomation by producing antibodies that combat the toxic components—the first time the person is stung! That is the good news. The bad news is that any additional envenomation by a scorpion with identical or very similar toxins may sensitize the individual (make the person acutely allergic). Sensitizing may take several stings. An individual cannot tell until he or she is envenomated again. A sensitized person will likely have an anaphylactic reaction to subsequent envenomations, possibly violent and life threatening. In a worst-case scenario, the victim stops breathing, suffers heart failure, and dies, all in a few minutes. No, this is not overly melodramatic.

Statistics show that many more people die of anaphylactic shock resulting from arthropod bites and stings than by the toxic effects of the venom. This holds true with scorpions. If you are highly allergic to some medicines and to bee, wasp, or ant stings, you **may be** highly susceptible to developing a scorpion venom allergy as well.

stings should be treated like any small stab wound, and care should be taken to clean the wound and apply an antiseptic.

The Great Fear— A Serious Reaction

Small children, the elderly, and people with impaired or weakened immune systems, serious preexisting medical conditions, or hypertension

Antivenin

Scorpion antivenin (antiserum that combats the effect of venom) is produced at a few laboratories throughout the world. Like polyvalent antivenin produced for pit vipers, a few types of scorpion antivenin seem to work on several different types of scorpion venom. A variety of antivenin is produced, mostly for the more dangerous scorpions found in a particular region. For

Buthacus arenicolor are extremely fast, delivering relatively potent venom in a series of rapid strikes, and are only for advanced keepers.

example, *Androctonis* antivenin does not work on *Tityus* envenomation. There is considerable debate about the efficacy of using antivenin because so few scorpion stings are actually life threatening and antivenin itself has the potential of producing a serious allergic reaction. In most cases of scorpion envenomation, the antivenin is more dangerous than the venom it is treating. Most antivenin is produced by injecting horses with small doses of venom and extracting the immune bodies produced in their blood. The reaction to the horse serum can cause anaphylaxis.

Experiments are being made to produce scorpion antivenin by using goats rather than horses. Until recently, the venom lab at Arizona State University had produced scorpion antivenin from goats for many years, which seemed to be safe and effective for *Centruroides* envenomation. Currently, this type of antivenin is being pro-

duced in Mexico, where envenomation from the genus *Centruroides* is more extensive and acute.

A Desensitizing Treatment

A person sensitized to scorpion venom can undergo a long-term (24-month) desensitizing regimen similar to one that has been effectively used by people allergic to bee and wasp stings. The regimen includes weekly injections of increasingly larger amounts of venom followed by monthly maintenance doses. Obviously, such a procedure should be reserved for someone who must work with scorpions on a daily basis. On rare occasions, or if you are really lucky, continued stings may stimulate your body to build stronger-than-normal immunities to the toxins. Do not try to do this on your own! You must consult an allergist.

Venom Extraction Devices

For many years, dozens of devices that suck venom out through the wound have been manufactured. All have had inadequacies, usually in the amount of suction that they produce. Also, it was thought that there was a need for cutting the wound in order to compensate for the inadequate suction.

Some data suggest these devices are effective in removing a small quantity of venom, provided they are applied almost immediately, before the body has transported the venom away from the envenomation site. Some experienced medical personnel and toxicologists recommend the currently produced device The Extractor as immediate first aid for venomous arthropod stings.

Many arachnid keepers question the value of The Extractor, mostly because of the skepticism remaining from previous designs and their somewhat cavalier approach to being stung. Although most scorpion stings do not require medical attention, there is no harm in using The Extractor. Anything that will alleviate some of the pain and reaction of a scorpion sting seems a sensible course of action. The kit is available at most sporting goods and outdoor stores.

Buthacus leptochelys nitzani is quick in attempting to escape and is just as quick to deliver venom with a barrage of rapid stings.

COMMONLY AVAILABLE SCORPIONS

Hundreds of thousands of scorpions are imported into the United States each year, with an undocumented number going to Europe. Many die in transit; perhaps as little as 25 percent will survive their first year in captivity. Poor husbandry is the greatest cause of this high mortality rate.

At the Pet Shop

Most first scorpions are purchased at a pet shop. Advanced keepers are almost always very specific in the species of scorpions they collect. They buy from private arachnid breeders, either directly or at reptile and arachnid shows and meetings held periodically throughout the United States and Europe.

This growing network of scorpiophiles has gained an astounding amount of knowledge about the natural history of their animals in order to keep the scorpions in the best-possible condition. The majority are young (late teens to 30s) and keep an assortment of species that they breed to trade or to sell surplus animals to others sharing their interest. Scientific names are almost always used when corresponding, so

An exceptionally patterned 4th instar female Centruroides sculpturatus.

the neophyte should learn the terminology. These scientific names can be located through arachnid-related chat rooms and web sites where individuals freely share their husbandry accomplishments. Scorpiophiles very commonly expand into other arthropod-keeping areas, most commonly tarantulas.

Once you have done the proper preacquisition research and have decided to purchase a scorpion, preparations should be made for housing and feeding before bringing it home. If the cage is purchased at the same time as the scorpion, you should have a good idea of what you will need. Selected species are discussed in depth later.

What to Look For

The primary consideration when looking for the right scorpion is its health. An excellent clue is the conditions under which it has been kept.

- Is the cage substrate dirty?
- Are dead cricket or mealworm carcasses lying about? Molds and mites quickly contaminate a filthy cage, making it a totally unsuitable environment. A healthy scorpion will eat what it kills.
- Is a dish with clean water available?
- Has a hiding place been provided to allow the scorpion to hide from bright light and annoyances?
- Is the scorpion in a warm place? Most of the larger species prefer temperatures of 80°F (26.7°C) or higher and may be lethargic and refuse food if kept too cool.

Check the Animal's Physical Condition

- Is the scorpion alert and quick to run away or assume a defensive position when touched? This responsiveness is expected and normal. A pencil is a safe tool to use to test this.

- Does the animal seem lethargic, limply lying on the surface?
- Does it appear emaciated or overly thin? If so, ask that the scorpion be fed a cricket or mealworm. Likely, if it is simply underfed and not too cool or overly stressed, the scorpion will take the food immediately.
- Does it have all of its appendages? Unlike tarantulas, scorpions rarely regrow more than a small part of a severed leg.

If you are not satisfied with your evaluation or you have second thoughts, look for a different scorpion. A novice is not knowledgeable enough to save a sick or dying scorpion. Realistically, very few things can be done for such an animal. If we refuse to buy unhealthy scorpions, the money lost by pet shops will force changes in how they care for scorpions. They will also have to stop dealing in poor-quality livestock.

The Best "Pets"

A novice's first scorpion should be easy to acquire, inexpensive, simple to maintain, large, long-lived, not prone to sting, and have mild venom. An emperor scorpion, *Pandinus imperator,* is recommended as this best first choice. This species is quite tolerant and will allow the keeper to observe scorpion characteristics easily while learning the basics needed to provide it with an adequate environment, all with practically no potential of a dangerous envenomation.

The forest scorpion (*Heterometrus* spp.) is another widely available and easily kept scorpion that is physically very similar to the

A positive identification of **Pandinus cavimanus** *cannot be assured by the reddish coloration on its chelae, which is found on other* **Pandinus** *species.*

emperor scorpion. However, forest scorpions frequently have a different disposition, are quicker to defend themselves, and have a bit more toxic venom than emperor scorpions. Two species of forest scorpions (*H. spinifer* and *H. longimanus*) are so similar that they are commonly sold as the same animal. *Pandinus* and *Heterometrus* will use their large, powerful chelae to give a substantial pinch that is capable of breaking the skin and drawing blood in rare instances. They also live in hot, humid regions in moist ground litter and burrows. Therefore, they require some moisture to prevent their desiccation and death. One or more of these species are available year-round.

You should first become knowledgeable and successful at keeping these larger types of scorpions before you assume the responsibility of other more delicate and smaller forms. As the interest in keeping scorpions for a hobby grows, more and different species are being imported.

Scorpions for the Novice

The following recommended scorpions are weakly to mildly venomous, terrestrial, and not prone to climb. This makes them safer, easier to cage, and less likely to escape.

Emperor Scorpion
(Pandinus imperator)

As we have seen, the emperor scorpion (*Pandinus imperator*) is one of the best scorpions for the novice. It is large, shiny, and black with bumpy chelae. The mystique associated with an emperor scorpion, probably caused by

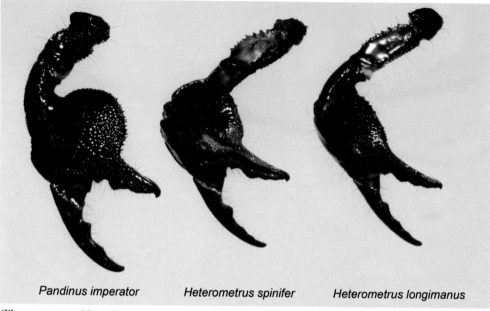

Pandinus imperator   Heterometrus spinifer   Heterometrus longimanus

These common black/brown scorpions may be identified by their chela.

its ominous, impressive appearance, is totally unfounded but makes it very attractive to potential scorpion enthusiasts. It is one of the least likely to defend itself by stinging, and its venom is mild. Prey is grasped and crushed by the scorpion's huge chelae. It is inoffensive, almost shy, preferring to run away or shield itself with its chelae. If cornered, however, it may assume a formidable defensive position and use its chelae to grab at the agitator. The grasp may be strong enough to draw blood from a person's finger.

Emperor scorpions have been the standby of the pet trade for many years. Hundreds of thousands (possibly millions) have been sold. With the recent increased interest in scorpions as pets, the annual number is constantly increasing. To limit overcollecting, a few coun-

tries in which this species is found have listed it and some other species with the Convention on the International Trade of Endangered Species (C.I.T.E.S.). This listing is designed to report the number of specimens that are exported from a specific country. Permits are required for businesses and persons to import C.I.T.E.S.-listed animals and plants.

Natural history: Emperor scorpions are native to hot, moist, tropical West Africa (Ghana, Togo, and other countries near the equator). They live near the surface in tunnels in moist leaf litter, along stream banks, and under moisture-retaining ground debris. They are frequently found in great numbers near human habitation. When prey is readily available, dozens can live in dense colonies, sharing an area of a few square yards, sometimes cohabiting in the same hole. This trait permits keeping several together in a communal cage.

Size: The emperor scorpion, known to reach an overall length of greater than 8 inches (20 cm), is erroneously claimed to be the largest living scorpion in the world. Some species of forest scorpions (*Heterometrus* spp.) are its equal. Pregnant female emperor scorpions can be massive, weighing more than 1 ounce (28 g). Because of their amazingly long metasomas, male flat-rock scorpions (*Hadogenes* spp.) attain greater lengths, but they are considerably less robust. *The Guinness Book of Records* claims a forest scorpion native to rural India, *H. swammerdami*, to be the largest scorpion in the world, 9 inches (23 cm) in length. If this record is valid, it must be a unique and very, very impressive and formidable specimen. In contrast, one of the ten species of *Microtityus* is possibly the smallest scorpion in the world. However, most arachnologists believe the 0.5-inch (12 mm) Oaxaca, Mexico, ground-litter-inhabiting *Typhlochactas mitchelli* is the tiniest.

Pandinus is a wide-ranging Central African genus that noticeably avoids arid areas. Only two of the 24 species are available in the pet trade. The Tanzanian red-clawed scorpion (*P. cavimanus*) has similar body structures to *P. imperator* but is slightly smaller, quicker in its movements, and noticeably more defensive. It usually has maroon-colored pedipalps, from which it has gotten its common name.

Other *Pandinus* species are more difficult to identify because many of them have traits similar to the forest scorpions (*Heterometrus* spp.) described under the next heading. All *Pandinus* species live in fairly moist environments, but little has been reported about their natural history. However, no other known *Pandinus*

species is typically as docile and unwilling to sting as is the emperor scorpion.

Captive conditions: When emperor scorpions are housed together, care must be taken that the enclosure is big enough to avoid crowding. To prevent cannibalism, the animals should be similar in size and adequately fed. Even then, without warning, one may decide to make a meal of a cage mate. For a few days after a scorpion molts, its exoskeleton is very soft. Until it hardens, the animal is vulnerable to the attack of an aggressive cage mate.

Forest Scorpions
(*Heterometrus* spp.)

The expansive genus *Heterometrus* is constantly being revised and reassigned. It is a classification nightmare. Even if you know the country from which your specimen originated, accurately identifying the species is extremely difficult. They must be distinguished by

Heterometrus laoticus is found in humid environments.

Water

Although many scorpions appear to survive without water, as a precaution, a shallow dish of clean water should be offered periodically. The frequency depends upon the environment from which the particular species originated. Adding pea-sized gravel to the shallow water dish will prevent drowning.

anatomical characteristics that are best seen through a dissecting microscope.

Natural history: Forest scorpions range from India westward throughout southern Asia and Malaysia. Two species, the East Indian forest scorpion (*H. longimanus*) and its many subspecies and also the Thailand forest scorpion *(H. spinifer)* are the most commonly obtainable. Occasionally, the Indian forest scorpion (*H. fulvipes*) is available, but exportation from that region is sporadic.

Description: All are large, stocky, heavy, dark scorpions that look very much like emperor scorpions and are frequently misidentified and sold as that species. The problem is compounded because *Pandinus* and *Heterometrus* are closely related. Adult *Heterometrus* have slender and smoother chelae than *P. imperator* and *P. cavimanus*. Although most are black, some individuals of both genera are a rich, chocolate brown, and others have a green or blue sheen when viewed in bright light.

Defensiveness: Forest scorpions differ from emperor scorpions in their greater readiness to assume a defensive posture and protect themselves by using their chelae and telsons. Also, they are noticeably quicker, running in rapid short spurts. Fortunately, most people's reaction to the venom of most Heterometrus species is only slightly more discomforting than that from an emperor scorpion.

The similarity with *Pandinus* continues in that they both prefer a moist, tropical forest environment and frequently live communally. A large cage and adequate feeding are necessary to maintain a group. However, this can be problematical because they are more territorial than *Pandinus*, and cannibalism is always a distinct possibility.

Identification: One would assume that if the origin of the animal is known, identification is less difficult. This may not be as easy as it seems because most exporters use common names. (They rarely, if ever, know valid scientific names). Additionally, the animals have changed hands several times since they were captured. Importers ship to jobbers, who may ship to distributors, who ship to pet shops. Also, to many of the parties involved, a large black scorpion is simply that—a large black scorpion! Important identification characteristics are the size and shape of the chelae and granulations on the carapace.

Scorpions for Experienced Keepers

After you have become comfortable with scorpions, are adequately supplying the needs of your charges, and understand the commitment you have made, you may start thinking about keeping some of the more delicate and demanding species. The following are available regularly, slightly more expensive, and offer

The compressed shape of Hadogenes paucidens *permits it to fit in snug spaces.*

greater husbandry challenges than *Pandinus* or *Heterometrus.*

Flat-rock Scorpions

(*Hadogenes* spp.)

The common name, flat-rock scorpion, aptly describes a unique genus of African scorpions (*Hadogenes*). They are distinctly flat with very long, incredibly thin metasomas. Their shape enables them to live in the narrow spaces between rocks.

Natural history: The majority of this genus lives in South Africa and cannot be legally exported. Occasionally, dealers offer specimens labeled as *H. bicolor,* but its identity and legitimacy are questionable because it is a South African species. Two forms that range into Rhodesia and Mozambique, *H. paucidens* and *H. troglodytes,* are commonly found in the pet trade.

Description: *Hadogenes* are large to very large but not heavy bodied or massive, like *Pandinus* or *Heterometrus.* The maximum recorded overall length of a male *H. trogodytes* is 8.3 inches (21 cm). Their large, strong, elongated pedipalps and flat chelae add to the flattened contour and are well adapted for grabbing prey hiding in cracks and fissures. Their wide, flattened pedipalp surfaces serve

═══ CAUTION! ═══

Not for Novices!

A novice should never attempt to keep any of the scorpions described in this section.

as shields, blocking the entrance to their retreat. At first sight, these scorpions are so flat that they appear to have been squashed.

Defensiveness: Many flat-rock scorpions are slow to run, docile, and rarely sting. Their venom ranks among the lowest in toxicity of all scorpions, causing little if any reaction in humans. These attributes make them highly desirable to the novice keeper, but they are more delicate than emperor scorpions and forest scorpions.

Captive conditions: *Hadogenes* require dry cages with a carefully arranged and secured stack of rocks or slate providing several narrow, tight-fitting hiding places. Because they are territorial, they should be kept alone. Although they rarely drink, a shallow container of fresh water should be provided once a month. Flat-rock scorpions are seasonally available, some-times in short supply. They are more expensive than *Pandinus* or *Heterometrus*.

African Burrowing Scorpions
(*Opistophthalmus* spp.)

Natural history: There are approximately 50 species of African burrowing scorpions (*Opistophthalmus*) ranging throughout the southern and eastern third of Africa. Most reside in South Africa. Nearly all are obligate burrowers, preferring friable but fairly hard-packed, sandy soils in which they can dig relatively long, deep tunnels.

Description: Species vary in size from 2.5 inches (6.5 cm) to 5 inches (12.7 cm). Large numbers of three large species, yellow-legged burrowing Scorpion (*O. glabifons*), and Tri-colored burrowing scorpion (*O. ecristatus*) and Wahlberg's burrowing scorpion (*Opistophthalmus wahlbergi*) are usually imported. All three have stocky builds and large, broad chelae, giving them a solid appearance. Also, they are more colorful than are any of the previously mentioned forms. They are mostly light shades of tan and yellow.

Captive conditions: Large females are impressive, attractive scorpions. Unfortunately, they spend most of their lives hidden underground in their burrows, so they are inconspicuous captives.

Defensiveness: All species will sting readily if cornered or restrained. One species, *O. carinatus*, is said to have potent venom, while the others vary from mild to powerful. Regardless of the species, *Opistophthalmus* envenomation is intensely painful at the site of the sting for

Opistophthalmus wahlbergii is frequently confused with O. boehmi.

Hadrurus spadix requires a mostly dry enclosure with sand substrate in which to dig.

as long as 48 hours but causes no lasting after-effects. The pain has been equated to that produced by bashing a finger with a hammer.

Giant Hairy Scorpions
(*Hadrurus* spp.)

Natural history: They live in rocky deserts where they dig deep burrows in dry sandy soil. Of the eight known species, the Arizona hairy scorpion (*Hadrurus arizonensis*) may ordinarily be found for sale. They are most commonly available in late summer, having been activated by the monsoon rains inundating the southwestern deserts at that time.

Another species, the black hairy scorpion (*H. spadix*), shares much of the same overall range in northern and western Arizona and southern Nevada, Utah, and California but is found farther north through Nevada into Oregon and Idaho. Its defining characteristics are a yellow metasoma and legs, with dark gray or black tergites and reddish chelae tips. A central and southern California and Mexican species, the California hairy scorpion (*H. obscurus*), is rarely available. Additional species are found in Mexico, but we need not be concerned with these because it is illegal to export any wildlife from that country.

Description: Giant hairy scorpions (*Hadrurus*) are the largest scorpions found in North America. Typical adults of both species range in size from 4–4.5 inches (10–11 cm), with exceptionally large specimens capable of reaching lengths in slight excess of 5 inches (12.5 cm). The common name of this genus refers to the prominent number of setae that are found over most of their bodies, legs, pedipalps, and telsons.

Defensiveness: This yellow-green scorpion is rather docile, rapidly running from a confrontation. However, it will assume a defensive position and sting if cornered and provoked. Its venom is considered weak to mild, but pain and swelling occur at the site of the envenomation.

Captive conditions: Because all giant hairy scorpions have nearly identical natural histories, they can be maintained under similar conditions. Although a large cage with a 12-inch-deep (30 cm) layer of dry, loamy sand is preferable, they do well in a medium cage with a 3–4 inch (7.5–10 cm) layer. In the wild, they have been found in burrows as deep as 6 feet (2 m). They spend a lot of time digging but will use a few flat stones or pieces of bark to hide under. They are territorial and must be kept alone. Otherwise, the result will inevitably be one fat scorpion.

For some unknown reason (probably an environmental factor relating to tunneling and moisture), captive-born young rarely survive more than a month or so. Also, the mother frequently cannibalizes them within a few hours to ten days of birth without noticeable provocation.

Very few early instars survive the ordeal of molting, and moisture seems to be a key factor. The lengthy subterranean part of their lives remains a mystery. However, it appears to be a very important variable in their natural history and healthy survival.

Adults are very easy to care for and the most desirable and widely kept scorpions indigenous to the United States. They are aggressive feeders who will gorge themselves when plenty of food is provided and then not feed again for an extended period. They are prone to fasts; healthy specimens have lived for six months without feeding. Hairy scorpions are long-lived, many having been kept for more than 15 years. Like other scorpions from arid environments, their liquid requirements are provided by their food. These are adaptations to surviving in a dry, harsh environment, where large numbers of prey animals and water are available for only very brief periods during the year. However, they drink readily in captivity and should be offered water periodically.

Gold Scorpion
(*Scorpio maurus*)

Natural history: Gold scorpions burrow in dark, sandy soils in rocky areas; hundreds of these burrows may be found in a section of ideal habitat. Smaller than any of the previously described species, they are frequently available and relatively inexpensive. The single species within the genus, *Scorpio maurus,* has been separated into as many as 19 subspecies by various taxonomists. They inhabit a large region of western Africa and the Middle East on into India. Additional study of the systematics of this species will likely result in changes. Some subspecies will become full species, and others will be eliminated. It is a classic example of the perplexing disarray that exists in scorpion taxonomy.

Description: The Egyptian gold scorpion (*S. maurus palmatus*) is the most commonly imported subspecies. This quick-moving, chunky, midsize scorpion, 2–3 inches (5–8.9 cm) in length, has a shiny, straw yellow or golden yellow body and legs with dark tips on its large chelae. With some imagination, the large, short, rounded chelae resemble boxing gloves.

Defensiveness: Although their venom is considered mild, the toxicity varies considerably among the subspecies. An envenomation is quite painful, with some subspecies producing more severe symptoms than others. Temperament also varies. Certain specimens will readily sting if confronted, but all will grab at the annoyance with their strong chelae. Because of their disposition and the pain associated with a sting, a novice should not keep gold scorpions.

Though capable of inflicting a painful sting, Scorpio maurus is easy to maintain and does well in captivity.

Captive conditions: With proper substrate and adequate food, a group of six to eight can be successfully kept in a 10-gallon (37.8 liter) aquarium that has been set up as a terrarium. Several small, flat rocks placed about the surface will enable each scorpion to build its own hiding spot. Tunnel entrances and scrapes are usually built alongside or under a rock.

These scorpions are very strong for their size. When digging burrows, they easily move pebbles and small rocks, sometimes those larger than they are. At night, they stand outside of their retreats with extended pedipalps and open chelae, waiting to ambush passing insects. If this is ineffective, they will move about searching for prey.

Many keepers claim that these scorpions do not do well in captivity, rarely living longer than a year. Because most are caught as adults, it is likely that they simply have a shortened life span. A life span of 2–4 years is common with most of the smaller scorpion species, while larger ones live 4–15 years or longer. A soil moisture gradient may possibly be needed within the burrow to improve survival. This gradient may be the key to keeping many desert taxa, particularly those that frequently have trouble shedding in captivity or seem to die spontaneously for no apparent reason.

Scorpions to Avoid

The rationale for the current trend to acquire more-toxic scorpions is unclear, but it appears to parallel that of snake keepers wanting to have very dangerous snakes. It is a psychological false assumption of machismo—bigger and "badder" demonstrate the keeper's ability to possess and confront danger. Why this mindset is so rampant is a complex subject that needs to be explored,

understood, and confronted fully before it causes a universal ban on keeping any exotic animals. Several cities and states have initiated laws overseeing the keeping of what legislators perceive to be dangerous animals and more are attempting to do so. The pet industry and keepers must find a way of educating or preventing unqualified people from acquiring animals that are a potential danger to themselves and others.

Many potentially lethal scorpions are available but should be left only to the most experienced keepers. Even they should think long and hard before taking on such a potentially dangerous responsibility. Scorpions are amazing escape artists and can hide in incredibly small spaces. This and the fact that they are nocturnal make escapees very difficult to find. Consider not only the threat to your own safety, but to that of others.

Bark Scorpions
(*Centruroides* spp.)

Natural history: Approximately 40 species (with as many as 24 subspecies) of bark scorpions are found throughout North America, Central America, northern South America, and the West Indies. They live in a variety of environments, ranging from arid deserts to moist forests. Those from deserts prefer a slightly moist niche within otherwise dry areas. They are found under loose bark, inside rotting cacti, in cracks and holes in trees, in bromeliads, among palm fronds, under leaves, under trash, under surface litter, and in rock piles—anywhere that maintains some moisture, provides shelter, and harbors prey. This includes houses—both rural and urban. In those regions where cattle are raised cow "patties" are commonly used for cover. Others may be found foraging after dusk in open sandy areas. They are

For years the showy gerschi *morph of the plainer* Centruroides sculpturatus *was thought to be a different species.*

excellent climbers, commonly observed above the ground in bushes and trees.

Bark scorpions are fast runners. Many species will sting at the slightest provocation. When first uncovered, they freeze. If touched, they respond immediately with a few rapid stings and then run out of sight, hiding in a crevice or other dark place. The majority of human envenomations occur from unseen scorpions. In most instances, these scorpions are accidentally encountered when they are clinging to the underside of a rock, bark, lumber, or other object where they are easily and accidentally grabbed.

Bark scorpions are very active nocturnal foragers. Because they are so mobile, they find their way into many unexpected places. In the Southwest, where they may be common inside houses, it is often said that if a scorpion is found climbing a wall or walking on the ceiling, it is *Centruroides*. They have been known to fall from the ceiling onto a sleeping person. Stories abound about them climbing into bedding, clothes, shoes, and other things in the human environment. Stepping on one, while walking barefoot in a darkened house, is a common way of being stung.

Description: Bark scorpions are mostly small, but the elongated slender metasomas of the males of some species may give them slightly greater overall length. They are patterned and colored very much like their environment, which makes them difficult to see. Tropical species tend to be darker shades of brown, while those from arid areas are tan or yellowish.

Defensiveness: The potency of their venom varies greatly from species to species. As the commonly found species in Arizona, eastern New Mexico, southern California, and adjacent areas in Nevada and Utah, the Arizona bark scorpion *C. sculpturatus* is considered to be the most dangerous scorpion in the United States. It has caused deaths but is nowhere nearly as toxic as a few other bark scorpion species found in Mexico.

Although *Centruroides* envenomation is relatively common in the southwestern United States, the wide availability of doctors, hospitals, and antivenin has all but eliminated deaths. In fact, none have been recorded in the United States since 1968. Current emergency medical treatment for stings of *C. sculpturatus* does not include antivenin.

A few Mexican and other Latin-American species are extremely dangerous. Indigent people are prone to frequent encounters because of their lifestyle. Thousands of deaths from bark scorpions used to occur annually in Mexico, mostly from *C. elegans, C. infamatus, C. noxius,*

A long, thin telson reveals this **Centruroides margaritatus** *to be male.*

C. suffusus, and *C. limpidus.* In the past few years, the availability of antivenin, combined with education and eradication programs, has dramatically lowered the annual mortality rate into the low hundreds. Still, as many as 800 deaths are attributed to 100,000 envenomations annually.

The wide-ranging slenderbrown bark scorpion, *C. gracilis,* is frequently available in the pet trade. Those specimens collected in Florida have mild venom, but others from Central America are more toxic. Like most bark scorpions, they are quick to defend themselves and envenomations are common. The most unusual reported sting (actually several stings) was to a professional football player in Phoenix who was dressing for a game and partially crushed an Arizona bark scorpion that was hiding in his jersey. The player received antivenin (probably totally unnecessary) and played in the game without further problems.

Centruroides envenomation causes reactions ranging from minor discomfort to prolonged severe pain and a burning sensation at the site that dissipates within a few hours. It is important to caution that very little is known about the effects of the venom of many bark scorpion species. To avoid problems, less-experienced keepers should not attempt to maintain exotic *Centruroides* species that are occasionally imported from Central America.

Captive conditions: *Centruroides* prefer a sand/potting soil mixture as a substrate with many pieces of bark and flat stones as places in which to hide. The environment should be slightly moist (barely damp, not wet), with dryer areas available. A light weekly misting is recommended. Those from tropical regions prefer a greater percentage of moisture-retaining substrate. Vertical pieces of layered bark or similar material must be provided as hides because these scorpions frequently climb and almost always molt at a slightly downward angle.

They do well communally if well fed and kept in a sizable cage. A tight-fitting lid is a must as they are excellent climbers and are incredibly adept at escaping through the smallest cracks. Care must be taken when lifting ground objects because bark scorpions frequently hang upside down on these items.

Death Stalker
(*Leiurus quinquestriatus*)

Natural history: Native to the rocky desert regions of arid North Africa and the Middle East, the death stalker spends the daylight hours in burrows and scrapes it has cleared under ground litter and rocks. Abundant in some areas, it is frequently seen at night actively searching for small invertebrates on the ground, on stone walls, and in bushes. Although it may occasionally enter a house, it is most frequently seen in rural areas where prey is prevalent. Currently, three species (*L. quinquestriatus*, *L. jordanensis*, and *L. savanicola*) are very wide-ranging. Three subspecies have been described.

Description: *L. quinquestriatus* is medium sized, 3.5–4.0 inches (9–10 cm), with a sleek, tan body; pale, greenish yellow legs; and long, thin pedipalps and metasoma (except for the much darker fifth segment). Its nondescript appearance gives it a convincingly graceful, innocuous appearance, similar to many scorpions living in arid regions throughout the world. Do not be misled. The death stalker is fast moving and unpredictable. It may inject extremely potent venom with the slightest provocation.

Defensiveness: In North Africa, *L. quinquestriatus* causes 85 percent of the reported envenomations and 90 percent of the scorpion sting deaths. Because few victims of death stalker stings have the initial symptoms usually associated with most serious scorpion envenomations—pain, muscle contractions, excessive salivation, respiratory irregularity, twitching and convulsions, an unstable pulse rate, and erratic

This African scorpion, Leiurus quinquestriatus, is a potentially deadly arachnid to keep.

body temperature—the seriousness of a sting is often initially underestimated. If not properly cared for, the patient may go into shock, develop progressive respiratory paralysis, have pulmonary edema (fluid in the lungs), and develop heart inflammation. The eventual result will likely be heart failure. Make no mistake— this is a very dangerous scorpion that is fully capable of killing adults (rarely). *Leiurus* venom is the most toxic venom of any scorpion known.

Fat-tailed Scorpion

(*Androctonus* spp.)

Natural history: Currently, 5 of the 13 species (with additional subspecies) of *Androctonus* are available in the pet industry. They are small to medium sized with a few that are occasionally larger. They are found from northern Africa into Pakistan and western India. The most venomous species is the large Tunisian fat-tailed scorpion, *A. australis*. It is found throughout arid northern Africa, frequently occurring in the same environment as *Leiurus*. It also lives in a burrow or scrape under rocks and ground litter but will inhabit loose sand as well. It is slow and deliberate in its movements but capable of quick, short bursts of speed when necessary. The slightest movement of air solicits a defense reaction. It can climb on rocks and other rough surfaces but seems to prefer a terrestrial existence. *Androctonus* is much more frequently found in urban areas and houses than *Leiurus*, posing a serious threat to humans.

Description: Specimens range in color from all yellow to yellow with black pigmentation on the last metasoma segment and chelae; some are matte black. At one time, these color variants were described as subspecies. They are approximately the same length as the *L. quin-*

Quick to react to the slightest confrontation, **Androctonus australis** *is capable of inflicting lethal stings to humans.*

questriatus, 2.5–4.0 inches (6.5–10 cm) but are not streamlined. Rather, they are considerably stockier with noticeably thicker metasomas. This thick metasoma is the reason for their common name, the fat-tailed scorpion. Simply stated, they look as potentially deadly as they are.

Defensiveness: *Androctonus* is not quite as potent as *L. quinquestriatus*. However, some species are capable of injecting larger quantities of venom, making them a serious threat to human lives. The toxicity of *Androctonus* has been equated to that of cobra venom.

Two other occasionally imported species in this genus, *A. amoreuxi* and *A. bicolor*, are dangerously toxic. *A. amoreuxi* is light colored, mostly yellow, and prefers sandy areas and dunes. It lives in a burrow it digs or in one dug by another animal. It also moves slowly when foraging but is extremely fast and quick if aroused.

Thin, elongated chelae and yellow "feet," contrasting with a dark olive-brown or black body, make *A. bicolor* easier to identify than *A. amoreuxi*. It is most common in areas of darker sand and soils, with rocky patches, where it lives in scrapes under large, flat stones and in animal burrows. It is more agile than the other *Androctonus* species and stings with little provocation.

Many of the troops stationed in Saudi Arabia are frequently stung by another species, *A. crassicauda*. Because of the troops' excellent physical condition, the incidents were considered minor and few were actually reported. However, it still must be considered a potentially dangerous scorpion.

Like the majority of scorpions, fat-tailed scorpions are sit and wait ambush predators. They ascend to the entrance of their hideouts at dusk to sit, with open chelae, awaiting an unfortunate passing small animal. All scorpions will forage if they need to.

African Thick-tailed Scorpions

(*Parabuthus* spp.)

Natural history: African thick-tailed scorpions live in a variety of hot, arid, sandy, and gravelly environments throughout southern and

eastern Africa. Various species have adapted to different habitats. Some are obligate burrowers, while others are not. Females burrow more frequently and more extensively than males. Burrows may be very long but barely a few inches below the surface, and they follow a spiral course. A few species inhabit sand dunes. Despite habitat preferences, all *Parabuthus* species live in arid environments.

Although most thick-tailed scorpions live in South Africa and few are exported, those from nearby countries more commonly make their way into the pet trade. The Mozambique fat-tailed scorpion, *P. mossambicensis*, is frequently available. Specimens of *P. leiosoma* and *P. transvaalicus* are seen with regularity. *P. villosus* is the largest buthid. It is rare in the pet trade but is seen in small numbers in the collections of advanced enthusiasts, mostly in Europe.

Description: *Parabuthus* is the last major group of Old World, potentially dangerous, mid-size-to-large scorpions (3.5–6.5 inches/9–16 cm) that are found in the pet trade. Their characteristically thick metasomas and stocky shapes make them easy to confuse with *Androctonus*. A major difference is that most, if not all, thick-tailed scorpions can make noise by stridulating when aroused.

Their coloration is as variable as their choice of habitats. Some species are black and others light tan or yellow, with a range of combinations and shades in between. It is important to note that color is not a primary characteristic in defining species. Color variations are a common phenomenon in a taxon that inhabits an area with soil or rocks of different types and hues.

Parabuthus transvaalicus *is known for envenomating thousands of people.*

This small, adult male Tityus falconensis is poised on a colorful fallen leaf.

The scorpion is less likely to be seen because it blends in, its color acting as camouflage.

Defensiveness: Although their venom varies in potency, unsubstantiated deaths from at least three species, *P. transvaalicus, P. capensis,* and *P. granulatus,* have been reported. The last species has the most toxic venom but has a very limited range and is not found in larger cities. To date, P. granulatus never enter the pet trade. Small numbers of *P. liosoma, P. mossambicensis, P. transvaalicus,* and rarely, *P. villosus* are exported from Mozambique, Namibia, and North Africa. Regardless of the potency, a sting has serious consequences—intense localized pain, stiff joints, general paralysis, and a variety of debilitating systemic effects.

The black thick-tailed scorpion, *P. transvaalicus,* is the most unusual looking species. A somber, matte black color; heavy, stocky body; and thick metasoma give it a nasty appearance. It can be defensive and quick to sting. It also has powerful venom. When irritated, it assumes an imposing defensive position and stridulates by rubbing the sharp tip of the aculeus on special rough-textured areas on the last mesosomal segment of the body and the first, second, and sometimes third segment of the metasoma, producing a raspy, clicking sound.

If this is not enough, some *Parabuthus* species have been reported to possess the ability to spray venom as a unique defensive tool. When further provoked, the scorpion continues to stridulate, which seems to charge the glands in its telson. It elevates its metasoma above its body and squirts a fine mist of venom as far as 3 feet (1 m) at the annoyance. Unsubstantiated records state the venom has been shot as far as 6 feet (2 m).

Venom sprayed into an eye is extremely painful and can possibly cause semipermanent damage. Needless to say, any encounter with *P. transvaalicus* should not be taken lightly.

Devil Scorpions
(*Tityus* spp.)

Although only recently for sale in the United States, the potential danger of several *Tityus* species makes them worthy of being singled out. To date, seven *Tityus* species out of the 170 are known to have produced fatalities in humans.

Natural history: Devil scorpions live in a microhabitat comparable to that of tropical bark scorpions, and almost any slightly damp area is habitable. Because of the similarity, many scorpiophiles call them bark scorpions as well. *Tityus* have been known to reach incalculably large numbers in older urban areas, where they thrive under houses and amid the rubble and trash associated with dilapidating neighborhoods. They climb well, and some species are considered to be mostly arboreal. Banana plants and palms offer ideal habitats. These scorpions pose a serious problem to agricultural workers.

Description: *Tityus* are the most speciose buthid. The 170 species are small (1–3.75 inches/ 2.4–9.5 cm) and most closely resemble *Centruroides* in shape and coloration. They range throughout the West Indies and both Central and South America. A primary identifying feature is the small-to-large pointed, secondary projection on the telson: the subaculear tubercle.

Defensiveness: Their disarmingly diminutive size, ability to be overlooked, and quickness to sting make them a serious potential threat wherever they are found. Most are moderately venomous, but a few are responsible for high rates of mortality. In Brazil, *T. serrulatus* causes more than a hundred deaths a year. Another Brazilian species, *T. bahiensis* is responsible for a number of deaths, while Trinidad and northern Venezuela have *T. trinitatis*, whose victims suffer hypersensitivity, localized pain, high fever, profuse sweating and salivating, difficulty

in swallowing, vomiting, numbness of the limbs, muscle contractions, and convulsions. In extreme cases, there is a loss of consciousness, with the victim lapsing in and out of a coma. The symptoms may persist as long as a week. Reactions are similar to those of the most venomous species of bark scorpions. It is obvious that many *Tityus* species deserve their common name, devil scorpion.

Captive conditions: *Tityus* species do well when kept in relatively moist conditions, like tropical bark scorpions, and should have the cage misted periodically to prevent desiccation. Layered vertical hides provide shelter. Be very careful though—they are proficient at escaping through any small cracks in cage lids.

Common Scorpions in the United States

With the exception of *Centruroides vittatus* occurring along the banks of the Mississippi River in Illinois, there are no scorpions in the Northeastern and upper midwestern states. If you live anywhere else in the contiguous United States, there is probably at least one species of scorpion living in your area. Approximately 100 different scorpion species and subspecies live in the United States. One, the northern scorpion (*Paruroctonus boreus*) makes its way into western Canada. Giant hairy scorpions (*Hadrurus* spp.) are the largest, with the others being midsize or smaller. Only the Arizona bark scorpion (*C. sculpturatus*) is known to have caused human deaths. This species is common, fre-

In a cluster of screw bean mesquite pods, this male **Centruroides vittatus** *is easily overlooked.*

quently encountered, and responsible for hundreds, perhaps thousands, of stings (but no recent deaths in the United States) annually.

The common striped bark scorpion (*C. vittatus*) has become established way out of its range in some southeastern cities. At least three small, isolated colonies are known in North Carolina, interestingly adjacent to barbecue restaurants. Apparently, the colonies' founders were sequestered in loads of mesquite wood transported from Texas. Without a doubt, additional colonies that have followed the same route will be discovered.

Eastern Bark Scorpions

Three other weakly to mildly venomous *Centruroides* are found in the southeastern United States—the Florida bark scorpion (*C. hentzi*), the Bahamas bark scorpion (*C. guanensis*), and the slenderbrown bark scorpion (*C. gracilis*). The last is a dark brown, midsize species, 3.5–4.6 inches (9–11.2 cm) long, that is widely distributed throughout the Caribbean and Central America. It appears to have been introduced into Florida many years ago, likely in cargo. It has become established in many areas, mostly south of Gainesville. It is less likely to sting than the other indigenous Florida scorpions. When it does, the results are about equal to that of a bee or wasp sting.

The small, 1.75–2.75 inch (4.4–7 cm) *C. guanensis* is limited (in the United States) to the three southernmost counties in Florida. It was quite likely introduced from a part of its island range: Cuba, the Dominican Republic, Haiti, or the Virgin Islands. The smaller *C. hentzi*, 1.5–1.75 inches (3.8–4.4 cm), ranges statewide (except in the southern Keys), and into extreme southern Georgia and Alabama. Isolated, probably intro-

Florida and southern Alabama and Georgia are the extent of the range of Centruroides hentzi.

duced colonies have been located in North and South Carolina. These three species are a minimal threat to healthy adults, causing usually nothing more than local pain and burning that may last a few hours at the site of a sting.

Western Scorpions

The southwestern United States is a veritable scorpion paradise with a wide variety of families and species. Occasionally authors list the numbers of forms differently depending upon their choice of taxonomic assignments. Although taxonomists regularly are reclassifying or describing new species, it is relatively safe to assume the following. California can boast 59 forms and Arizona is second with 41. Texas and New Mexico have 20, followed by Nevada with 16 and Utah with 13. To the northwest, Idaho has 6, Oregon 4, Washington 3, and Colorado 7.

The other western and central states each have at least one species.

Striped-tailed Scorpions

(*Vaejovis* spp.)

The complex genus *Vaejovis* contains as many as 60 species. They live in a diversity of habitats throughout the southeastern and southwestern states, Mexico, and as far south as northwestern Guatemala. The common name—striped-tailed scorpion—is somewhat of a misnomer. Some members of the genus do not have stripes on their metasomas. The genus is divided into several closely related species groups that are currently being reassessed. Many changes in their classification are being made, including new species and possibly new genera. *Vaejovis* do well as captives if they have some moisture available. Unfortunately, like nearly all of the small scorpions, they are short-lived, rarely surviving a fourth year. After reaching adulthood, some may live only one year. Because of their small size, shape, and habits, they are frequently misidentified as the more venomous bark scorpions.

One species, the southern unstriped scorpion (*V. carolinianus*), is the only scorpion in Virginia and Kentucky. It ranges widely in the southern Appalachian region of Georgia, South Carolina, and Tennessee and in northeastern Alabama. This small scorpion, 2–3 inches (3.7–5.1 cm) in length, varies in adult size and coloration (from tan to dark brown) throughout its range. Many colonies contain only small adults. Its slender build and secretive habits make it appear less prevalent than it is. In some areas, it is abundant in rock and woodpiles, under loose bark, in rotten logs and stumps, and in almost every other similar woodland niche that provides some moisture and food. It is very fast, choosing to run and hide when uncovered. It will readily sting, but envenomation is usually less painful than that of a bee or wasp.

Other American Scorpions

A visit to a local zoo, museum, or nature center should provide some ideas of where to look for scorpions and some information on their natural history. Science teachers and agricultural agents are also good sources of information. Perusing the publications listed in the

Vaejovis spinigerus *does well in a mostly dry cage.*

back of this book or going online to one of the web sites will produce a plethora of data and uncover helpful reference materials. Remember that the interest in scorpions is in its infancy. Much, much more needs to be learned.

The names of the United States' taxa read like a tongue-twisting Latin lesson. Aside from the previously described genera—*Centruroides*, *Hadrurus*, and *Vaejovis*—there are *Anuroctonus*, *Diplocentrus*, *Paruroctonus*, *Pseudouroctonus*, *Serradigitus*, *Smeringurus*, *Superstitionia*, *Uroctonites*, and *Uroctonus*. Most are small, relatively nondescript, and difficult to identify accurately, and they offer challenges to the keeper.

An International Traveler

The small lesser brown scorpion, *Isometrus maculatus*, has become established in various tropical and subtropical port cities throughout the world over the past 250 years, almost certainly accidentally carried in shipborne cargo. When discovered in many cities, it was misidentified, assumed to be a new species and described as dozens of other genera. It is believed to have originated somewhere in Asia. In the United States, it has been reported from the Florida Keys and coastal southern California. It is established on a few of the Hawaiian Islands and is assumed to be the only scorpion found there.

Educating Yourself About Scorpions

You should learn the basic techniques of keeping scorpions by acquiring one or more

Pseudouroctonus glimmei *lives under rocks and ground litter in the coastal mountains of California.*

of the novice species listed earlier before you attempt keeping the smaller, generally more delicate species. When you are confident that you are successfully maintaining healthy scorpions, you should go into the field to look for

The mountains of southeast Arizona, southern New Mexico, and southwestern Texas are home to **Pseudouroctonus cashi.**

Southeast Asia's Isometrus maculatus *has stowed away in cargo and established colonies in ports throughout the world.*

native species. A great deal can be learned about the habits of a species by observing the habitat in which it lives.

- Does it live in open, sandy areas or among grasses?
- Was it found under a rock or bark, in leaf litter, on the surface, or in a burrow?
- Did it climb to its hiding place?
- Was the microhabitat dry or moist?
- Were several specimens living communally?

Collecting Scorpions

Walking through a brushy desert, using only ultraviolet (UV) light to pierce the blackness of the night, is like opening a door to a mysterious, magical world. As your eyes acclimate to the eerie bluish magenta luminescence, nearly everything becomes monochromatic, difficult to discern. Shadows produced by plants, rocks, and debris assume a soft, surreal aura. An array of flying insects that would normally go unnoticed

annoyingly flocks to the light. Moths become insidious, dive-bombing pests. Each white, humanmade piece of litter (particularly plastic bottles) glows with a piercing brilliance, forcing you to squint to avoid its jarring radiance.

Eventually it happens—your eyes lock on to the unmistakable, luminous, blue-green form of a scorpion several feet away. You move toward it, mesmerized, enchanted by the ghostly vision. After applying a swift but gentle sweep with your forceps, you grab it by its telson, lift it from the ground, and hastily place it into a small, clear, plastic container. Bathed in the light of your flashlight, you examine the magnificence of your prize. For a brief time, you are absorbed; you gloat at your success. After turning off the flashlight, you reacclimate to

TIP

What to Carry in the Field

Always carry a flashlight with fresh batteries as a normal light source and a small pocket light is a smart addition as a backup. Have a partner as a safety factor, and enjoy sharing the experience. A fanny pack, small backpack, or vest designed for fishermen or photographers (with pockets everywhere) makes carrying containers, spare forceps, a bottle of water, a flashlight, spare batteries, a compass, an Epipen, and other things you might want, effortless.

A scorpion collector's dream is discovering a communal site of **Centruroides vittatus** *under a piece of bark with blacklighting.*

the UV light and continue the quest. There will be many more such pleasurable incidents that night. Each capture is its own reward.

The previous description is one of the extraordinary attractions of collecting and keeping scorpions.

The availability of portable UV lights (black lights) has made scorpion hunting fun and very rewarding. For the past few years, compact, self-contained, battery-powered UV fluorescent lights have been made for fishermen. They were designed to simplify baiting hooks at night when using monofilament line and produce a relatively safe, low-light-level UVA. They retail for approximately $25.00 and can be ordered through fishing catalogs or found at larger outdoor stores.

A much brighter professional fluorescent UVB light is sold through scientific supply houses. Type B ultraviolet light is potentially dangerous to the eyes and skin, and special glasses must be worn to prevent it from entering the eyes. The

UV light elicits an eerie blue-green fluorescence from **Pandinus imperator.**

fluorescent tube of this unit is larger. The heavy, cumbersome battery (made for a motorcycle) must be carried in a pack and attached with a wire. Its awkwardness, weight (5 pounds/2.3 kg), and much higher price ($180) make it less desirable for all but the most ardent hunters. Its biggest asset is that it lights a much broader area than other UV lights, permitting a quick, wide scan in open places.

In the past few years, extremely bright, tiny light-emitting diodes (LEDs) with UVB and UVC wavelengths have become available. A series of as many as 39 LEDs have been fitted into a high-quality metal flashlight head to produce an extremely bright UVB light. The relatively low battery drain enables three "C" cells to last as long as 8 hours. Smaller-size flashlights are being fabricated, but the larger ones produce the best results. A scorpion sitting out in the open will fluoresce brilliantly enough to be seen at a distance greater than 25 feet (7.6 m). A

headlight unit has three LED UV bulbs with a switch to an adjustable white bulb. A variety of sizes are being produced periodically.

Recently, another UV light source is being installed into the same three-C battery flashlight. It uses three CREE X UV bulbs. It is supposedly several times brighter than the units containing 39 UVB-LEDs or UVC-LEDs permitting collectors to see scorpions at nearly 100 feet (35 m). For some collectors, particularly those wishing to photograph scorpions at night in the wild, this is an advantage. All these units have trade-offs. Brighter ones use more power, which requires larger batteries that increase the weight and size. Also, they sell for $100–$250, making the investment appreciable.

The major drawback of UVB-LED, UVC-LED, and CREE units is eye damage that may be caused from looking directly into the light. This can be prevented by wearing special glasses that block some of the UVB and UVC emissions. A number of collectors find that extended viewing with UV causes headaches and minor imbalance. The light level, monochromatic rendering of nearly everything, or eyestrain from searching so intensely may be part of the cause.

Small, inexpensive, non-UV-LED or non-CREE X black light flashlights are available. They have tungsten (filament) bulbs that are coated to produce a UV–like wavelength. Unfortunately, they produce an inadequate glow from scorpions, rendering these flashlights all but useless.

Aside from white litter, most objects do not fluoresce. Instead, they simply blend into the monochromatic, bluish magenta light. Wearing snake-proof boots or canvas leggings (sold by outdoor suppliers) helps avoid injury from snakes and cacti. Also, you should stop periodically to maintain your bearings. It is very easy to get disoriented or lost when you are searching intently.

Avoiding Being Stung

Collecting scorpions always brings with it the possibility of being stung. Some precautionary measures should be taken. First and foremost, avoid physical contact with the scorpion. Although some arachnologists have few qualms about tailing scorpions (grabbing them freehand by their telson and the last segment of the metasoma), the procedure is unnecessary, fool-hardy, and quite possibly very dangerous.

A pair of 10-inch (25-cm), rubber-tipped forceps is the best all-around choice. They are available through most pet shops that sell scorpions and via mail order from scientific supply houses and some reptile dealers. For larger species, some collectors prefer steel kitchen tongs with soft rubber padding attached. When black lighting, paint the tips with fluorescent paint so that you can see exactly where they are relative to the scorpion. Incidentally, forceps are an excellent tool for removing cactus spines.

A variety of clear, small bottles are available in craft stores and hobby shops. Plastic bottles sold in coin shops are available in various sizes, and the bottles pharmacies place pills in are great. Be certain they are carefully washed to remove any residue.

To Collect or Not to Collect

In some localities, certain species may be extremely abundant. Not infrequently, turning over a piece of cardboard in a trash pile will expose a dozen *Centruroides vittatus* piled together, having been attracted by the moisture. In some plots of sandy desert, a hundred or more of *Smeringurus mesaensis* (formerly

---

━━ CAUTION! ━━

A Few Additional Cautions

When black lighting, you must move slowly and cautiously to avoid having a dangerous encounter with a venomous snake, a cactus, or any number of other stinging, stabbing, or tripping obstacles. More than one hunter has been painfully surprised by unknowingly disturbing an ant mound. This can have very serious consequences if they are harvester ants, *Pogonomyrex* spp. (the most toxic North American ant genus) or the red imported fire ant, *Solenopsis wagneri (invicta)*.

Paruroctonus) can be seen in a few hours. Occasionally, visiting a particular spot and being mindful to take just a few scorpions will not seriously endanger a population. Research has shown that a very small percentage of the inhabitants are on the surface at any given time. However, continuous, relentless collecting (as has been done in parts of Togo and Ghana with *Pandinus imperator*) can and will eventually eliminate the densest colony.

A collector must never take more scorpions than can be properly and adequately cared for. Be extremely careful to replace rocks, logs, bark, or any objects that are moved or turned in order to prevent irreparable habitat destruction. This is imperative where ground cover is minimal and moisture is at a premium. Be considerate so that some of our natural heritage survives to be enjoyed by our children and, hopefully, their children as well.

HOUSING AND THE IDEAL ENVIRONMENT

The scorpions that are most likely to be kept are found in three basic environments—moist tropical, semimoist grassland/savanna, and arid desert. Even meager attempts at duplicating their environment will provide suitable caging. Most scorpions are very adaptable and do not require elaborate setups.

A Secure Home

Spacious cages are unnecessary. In fact, they may be detrimental. Most scorpions are ambush predators with very small home ranges. They may have trouble finding and catching fast, mobile prey (like crickets) in a large cage. A dozen or more of some smaller communal species (for example, *Centruroides vittatus* and *C. gracilis*) can be kept in 15-gallon (57-L) terrariums provided there is a surplus of hiding places and they are fed adequately. The Scorpions may even breed. Regardless of the care taken, some cannibalism should be expected.

Scorpions are extremely adept at squeezing through small openings, agile enough to climb an array of objects, and strong enough to lift tops that are considered tight fitting. The

Central placement of the medial eyes shows this to be **Opistophthalmus boehmi.**

thought of having escaped scorpions colonizing your house is a traumatizing situation to all but the most dedicated naturalists.

Prevention and supervision are the best ways to insure their safekeeping. The first choices of most keepers are plastic terrariums and glass aquariums. They are fairly inexpensive, and a wide selection of sizes is available.

The Plastic Cage

Plastic terrariums are produced in sizes and depths to accommodate a variety of small animals and can be bought in any pet shop. The mini 4.4 × 7.1 × 5.5 inch (11 × 18 × 14 cm) terrariums will suffice for the smallest species. The small 6 × 9.1 × 6.6 inch (15.5 × 24 × 18 cm) terrariums are an excellent choice for small to midsize scorpions. The medium-large scorpions do better in the medium 7.7 × 11.7 × 8 inch (20 × 27 × 21 cm) cage. The large 8.5 × 14.5 × 10 inch (21.6 × 36.8 × 25.4 cm) sizes are fine for the largest scorpions and adequate for small community setups, but aquariums are better.

The all-plastic cages have an attractive, one-piece, clear, styrene bottom and sides and also a well-ventilated, tight-fitting top that snaps securely in place. A small, clear styrene door is affixed to the center of the top for safe access. If the slightly angled sides are kept clean, it is almost impossible for a scorpion to climb them.

Although nicely conceived and designed and good enough for many different types of animals, all-plastic cages have a few shortcomings worth mentioning, particularly when used for escape-prone scorpions. Clear styrene is not as durable as might be assumed. It is easily cracked, chipped, broken, and scratched if great care is not taken when cleaning it. Although the top has too many vents to retain much humidity for most scorpions, it is excellent for many arid-loving species. Gluing plastic or other material over some of the vented sections is the most practical way to increase humidity.

If space is at a premium, specially designed versions have tight-fitting, removable dividers that permit keeping a few scorpions in a condensed area. Although the bottom and sides are tight fitting, the gap at the top may provide enough space for a smaller, climbing species to visit its neighbor. This could lead to fatal results for one or both.

The Aquarium Cage

Glass sides and bottoms make aquariums heavier and susceptible to cracking. However, they are more rigid and sturdier than styrene cages and can provide years of service. The problem is acquiring a quality, tight-fitting top. Several tops are commercially produced for them, but these tops are designed for amphibians, reptiles, and small mammals. Most fit over the outside of the aquarium frame and are held on with a variety of clamping devices. Quite frankly, they are overpriced and fit too loosely, providing gaps that could be exploited by a scorpion escape artist. Also, they have an expanse of screening that prevents maintaining humidity. Plastic or nylon screening is totally unacceptable; scorpions may rip it with their chelae or "chew" right through it. In fact, some species will do their best to get through aluminum screening. Secure tops are addressed in the "How-To" section at the end of this chapter.

Alternative Cages

Scorpion keepers with large collections, limited space, or who are bent on captive breeding have learned to improvise without discomforting the animals, or becoming lax on safety. Literally hundreds of different-sized plastic containers can be easily modified to hold scorpions. The best ones are well made from flexible, quality plastic. They have tight-fitting, snap-on tops; are stackable; and have maximum ground surface with adequate height. Many keepers house entire collections in household plastic containers. These containers are not as attractive as aquariums and plastic cages, and the scorpions cannot be easily observed. However, they are practical and easier to maintain.

Small containers are the only sensible way of raising newborn scorpions that need to be kept individually. Round, plastic deli cups are available with snap-on tops. They are inexpensive, come in a variety of small sizes, and can be bought in quantity from restaurant suppliers or sometimes in small numbers from an obliging local restaurant. Rectangular refrigerator containers are

A heat tape affixed to the back wall of this shelf is an excellent heat source.

sturdier, are larger, offer more ground surface, require proportionately less shelf space, and have lids that are easier to remove and replace. Plastic containers made for storing shoes and sweaters are the next-larger choice. Avoid the clear acrylic plastic ones. They are brittle and will crack or chip with minimal stress.

The housewares sections of department stores stock a wide assortment of containers that will satisfy all your needs. Dollar stores are another source for a wide variety of containers at very reasonable prices.

A Light Source

Fluorescent light sources are available in different wattages and tube lengths. However, the compact, one-piece fixture made for kitchen undercounter use is inexpensive and an excellent size for most cages. Replace the standard bulb that comes with it with a safe black light (used to illuminate fluorescent paints and dyes) so you will have a light source for unobtrusively observing scorpions. Larger home and hardware stores and also poster shops frequently carry the tubes, or they can be ordered. Be sure that you do not mistakenly purchase one of the many bulbs

designed for raising plants. Scorpions do not seem to be overly effected by UV light, so they will carry on their nocturnal lives normally. The bulbs should not be kept lighted permanently. Use them to observe and feed the scorpions.

Normal (white) room light should be available for overall maintenance and cleaning cages. The ideal situation is to have normal lights on a timer to simulate or embellish a day and night cycle.

Labeling

A clearly visible plastic label with scientific name of the animal and a color-coded dot system identifies the species and goes a long way in preventing an accident. For instance, a red dot signifies a very dangerous scorpion. Yellow notes a quick, flighty, moderately venomous one. Green indicates a relatively innocuous specimen.

Cage Furnishings

Less is better! A simple cage setting is less problematic for the keeper and the scorpions. Scorpions simply do not need a lot of environmental dressing and, in fact, do better without it. A carefully prepared substrate, a few pieces of bark, a small flat rock or two, and a water dish (in some cases) are more than adequate. Live or plastic plants add nothing to the animal's well-being.

The Substrate

Substrate choice is a fundamental component in establishing a scorpion's captive environment and a key factor in keeping it healthy. The material used is important for all scorpions but it is an especially critical factor for fossorial ones. In nature, burrows offer protection from predators and weather and also provide a humidity gradient. Some species spend as much as 90 percent of their lives in these retreats. Females usually give birth there, some digging special birthing chambers. Newborns remain in the maternal burrow until their first molt and then disperse and dig their own.

Burrows range from a 1–2 inches (2.5–5 cm) to over 3 feet (1 m) in length, but the majority of them are 2–20 inches (5–50 cm). Exceptions occur. Adult *Hadrurus* species have been found as deep as 6 feet (2 m) in abandoned rodent tunnels. The density, compactness of the soil, and composition (amount of rock) determine how far they dig. Some scorpions solve the problem of very hard packed soil or collapsing tunnels by digging under plants in the root system or by using existing rodent and lizard burrows.

Tropical scorpions require proportionately higher humidity than desert forms and slightly more friable and damper substrate for burrowing. Those that dig burrows do well in a mixture of three parts potting soil and one part peat or mulch. Be certain that the soil does not have added fertilizers or chemicals.

Perlite or vermiculite can be mixed in to help retain water and keep the humidity high. These substances are fine to use because they are natural, lightweight, porous, inert, water-absorbing minerals. Either is frequently added to potting soil mixes. Perlite is a natural volcanic silicate (glass) that has been greatly expanded by being superheated. Vermiculite is mica that also has been expanded by being heated.

There are two aesthetic problems with these additives. First, they are lighter colored than the soil mixture. Second, when wet, the flakes stick to the scorpion's exoskeleton. When they dry, the flakes firmly adhere to the animal's surface, giving the scorpion an unnatural metallic sheen. In many cases, the substance remains until molting. This situation is particularly disturbing if the scorpion is an adult, because it will never shed again. Avoid mixes with small Styrofoam beads. They are very light in color and weight. As a result, they quickly come to the surface, making the cage unsightly. They are also poor at retaining moisture.

Regardless of the components of the substrate mixture, it should be soaked to moisten all the small particles, thoroughly squeezed until it is not sopping wet, and air-dried until it is just damp. Place it into the cage and press it until a compacted, 2- or 3-inch (5 or 7.5 cm) layer covers the bottom. Add an additional inch (2.5 cm) or so of friable mixture on top. If an appreciable amount of condensation forms after the cage cover is in place for a while, the substrate is too wet.

The inability to retain moisture is a major problem when keeping tropical scorpions in dryer areas, such as southwestern states. By simply increasing the depth of the substrate, evaporation is lessened considerably. Also, it should be watched and misted more frequently to assure some moisture is always present.

A series of tunnels excavated by **Hadrurus arizonensis.**

Desert scorpions: With the exception of sand-dwelling species, desert scorpions prefer somewhat densely packed, sandy soils into which they can burrow. Pet suppliers usually carry naturally orange sand from Utah (Jurassic sand) that has these properties. It is fairly expensive, mostly because of packaging and shipping, but may be the perfect, colorful substrate if you have only a few scorpions. Mixing it with 25 percent of other types of sand or potting soil does not overly weaken its consistency.

Be especially careful of where you collect sand. Avoid sand that is too close to heavily traveled roads or in areas that may have been sprayed with pesticides or herbicides. Chemical contamination can cause debilitating effects or even be lethal to scorpions. No matter where sand is acquired, wash it thoroughly to remove residual chemicals. Beach sand should be avoided because it may contain too much salt.

Basically, all you need is plain, old, desert sand and gravel, the kind that is not overly loose and that cakes when dry. You may be fortunate and find that the sand you have locally is perfect. However, be prepared to look elsewhere or improvise to get the consistency that compacts well and does not collapse when it is burrowed into.

Dry mixtures for burrowing: Bags of clean play sand, bought in the building departments of discount, do-it-yourself, and home stores, can be used as the basic ingredient. Without additives, though, it does not provide enough consistency for tunneling. Some keepers use high-quality potting soil sold as cactus mix.

One method of preparing a desert substrate is to mix thoroughly 1 part fine gravel, 1 part bentonite, and 12–15 parts fine-play or aquarium-grade sand. Bentonite is natural, porous, finely powdered aluminum silicate clay that is predominantly montmorillonite. There are two types, calcium bentonite and sodium bentonite. The latter one suits our purpose; it expands when moistened and forms a crust when dried. It is used by potters and well drillers as a binder and by masons to form the bottoms of naturalistic, outdoor, earth-bottomed fishponds. A small amount of bentonite goes a long way. Because it is abrasive, too much may scratch and excessively wear the exoskeleton. Although a supply may be difficult to find, it can be bought at some art supply stores that cater to potters and ceramic artists.

Another excellent, firm mixture is 5 parts quality potting soil, 10 parts sand, and 1 part bentonite. One part of finely chopped cypress mulch or peat can be included to add bulk and friability.

Ceramic makers have a number of additional sand and clay products at their disposal. With trial and error, some may be useful in keeping scorpions. One is grog, recycled previously fired clay that has been crushed and ground into different thicknesses. Medium or coarse grades blend nicely with sand and add bentonite for texture and binding. As a precaution, a painter's

mask should be worn when mixing any finely ground silica sands or compounds.

None of these percentages or methods is exact. A little experimenting may be needed to provide the most-fitting substrate for a particular scorpion species.

No matter what substrate you choose, as a preventative measure, wet and "nuke" it for several minutes in a microwave oven (on high setting) to kill any microorganisms. Ten or 15 minutes in a regular kitchen oven at 350°F (175°C) will probably do just as well. There is disagreement among arachnid keepers as to the value or need for nuking, but it cannot hurt.

Place the well-blended mixture into the cage. Thoroughly wet and tamp it into a lightly compacted state. Be sure it is nearly completely dry before introducing the scorpions.

Most other scorpions (grassland/savanna scorpions) can be kept in a soil that is a mixture of materials. Small cypress bark chips or mulch, peat moss, and pieces of sphagnum moss will thicken the substrate, while sand will make it more friable. Until you become an advanced scorpion keeper and can better evaluate their qualities and potential hazards, avoid using the exotic substrates sold for reptiles, amphibians, and other animals. Do not use mulches containing cedar, pine, or ground sugar cane or the treated, aromatic mulches claiming to maintain a fresh environment; some are lethal to arachnids.

Coconut husk: A product that is being used successfully by many arachnid keepers as a substitute for peat and cypress mulch is ground,

Bright, almost translucent yellow coloration makes **Buthacus arenicolor** *one of the more simplistically beautiful African desert scorpions.*

Paruroctonus silvestrii is very quick and prone to react to annoyance by striking an intruder.

dehydrated coconut husk. It is sold as a pet substrate and as a potting soil additive for gardeners. When soaked in hot water, the densely compressed brick expands to several times its mass. Not only does it hold moisture very well (which makes it excellent for *Pandinus* and *Heterometrus)*, but also it mixes with other materials to make them moisture retentive, friable, and thick enough to prevent burrows from collapsing. Adding various amounts of sand produces a variety of usable substrates.

Some fine tuning will be necessary because a scorpion's moisture needs vary greatly. Also, there is very little if any information about the requirements of many taxa that are periodically available. As a result, trial and error may be the only way to provide a suitable captive environment. Because the amount of moisture is vital, it should never be disregarded.

Starting a Burrow

Most species of scorpions can be induced to dig a burrow in a predetermined spot if a short section of tunnel entrance has been provided. Force a pencil onto the soil/sand, for a few inches at the edge of a stone or piece of bark, making a hole large enough to accommodate the scorpion. Many scorpions dig a scrape (a space beneath an object) as a refuge. The burrow must have a moisture gradient, ranging from an almost dry top surface to a slightly damp portion toward the deepest part of the substrate. With sand-dwelling scorpions, the upper sand should be kept dry to prevent caking on the scorpion's tarsi and to facilitate digging.

Water

Scorpions have managed to adapt and survive under a diversity of conditions in an amazing number of different environments throughout the world, but they are not invincible. It is a misconception that they do not need water. All animals need water to live.

Species inhabiting arid places may never need to drink water. In fact, many are highly susceptible to drowning if sprayed or by standing in as little as a few drops. They may not need free water. However, making it available for a few days every few weeks assures a source of potable water if they need to drink. Conversely, those from tropical and neotropical environments will die from desiccation if deprived of moisture. A constantly available supply of clean water is necessary for these scorpions. Distilled water should be used to eliminate any potential hazards of introducing chemicals that are used to purify our drinking water.

To maintain its elevated need for water, this **Heterometrus spinifer** *is actively drinking from its water dish.*

experimenting and observation will assure the best for the animal.

The safest way of maintaining a small collection of scorpions is to use slightly larger cages and maintain some moisture gradient. Taking care to keep a low moisture gradient on one side of the container is helpful for scorpions from the driest parts of the world as well. It provides an excellent all-around environment.

Doing some reading and asking more-advanced keepers is an excellent way of learning the basic needs of a species. A good clue to moisture requirements is the scorpion's overall color. Very dark (brown or black) animals with a shiny exoskeleton are almost always from moister habitats, while lighter ones (tan, yellow, and so on) are from arid places. Some species that live in dry areas are black, but their exoskeletons are usually dull black.

A New Water-Retaining Product

A recent product is available at pet suppliers as a unique, easy-to-use, safe, clean water source for crickets and other feeder insects. Several companies package it under a variety of trade names, but it is basically the same material—polyacrylamide copolymer. Randomly adding some small cubes of this premoistened gel into the substrate mix is more efficient for retaining moisture than perlite or vermiculite. It also will rehydrate when sprayed. Also, because there is no puddling, scorpions are not likely to drown. It does not evaporate as rapidly as water, so it maintains a moisture gradient while elevating humidity. A higher moisture level can

Very small, shallow clay or plastic dishes used under flowerpots are good water dishes for larger scorpions. Plastic bottle tops are excellent, small, serviceable water receptacles. Placing some clean gravel into the water will prevent scorpions and food animals from drowning. Using sponge or cotton is not recommended because they are difficult to keep scrupulously clean, dirty quickly, and become the vector of unsanitary bacteria and mold. A water dish with a wider surface area will evaporate more water, elevating the humidity. Putting a small one into a retreat is a great way to raise the humidity level. The scorpion will decide its moisture preference.

Moisture Gradient

The required amount of moisture and humidity varies widely, but some appears to be necessary for successful molting. Unless the keeper is sure of the scorpion's requirements, offering a moisture gradient in the cage is best. Some be maintained by adding a thin layer of the material into the substrate.

It comes in two versions, plain and with calcium. Arthropods apparently obtain no value from calcium, so the plain type should be chosen.

Nurseries sell a very similar product to provide a long-lasting water supply for potted plants. It comes as a gel or in a crystalline form and is less expensive. By adding water to the crystals, they are hydrated and expand into gelatinous bits.

Misting

Another method of assuring scorpions have an adequate supply of water is by judiciously spraying part of the cage periodically. *Pandinus*, *Heterometrus*, and other scorpion species from moister environments should be misted more frequently than all other forms. Great care must be taken to spray a small portion of the surface lightly in arid scorpion cages and not spray the animal directly. Spraying directly causes undo stress, and they may drown. Buy a new spray bottle rather than using one that used to contain any kind of chemicals.

Because many species are from places that receive the barest minimum rainfall, they have adapted to having little more than light dew a few times a year. The majority of the water comes from their food. They will seek out and harvest moisture from the surface. Some of these, mostly sand dune dwellers, will drown in any standing water.

A Trick for Retaining a Moisture Gradient

1. Cover the bottom of the cage with 0.5 inches (1.3 cm) of medium gravel, and add the substrate on top. Adding a thin layer of water-retaining crystals directly atop the gravel works well.

2. Cut the ends of a few plastic drinking straws at an angle, and push them vertically into the soil until they touch the cage bottom. Those with accordion bend sections can be bent at right angles to direct the flow away from the edges. Cut them off so that they protrude 1 inch (2.5 cm) or so above the surface.

3. Periodically, pour a very small amount of water into the opening. Capillary action will permit the water to migrate in the gravel and up in the sand, forming a gradient. Placing the pointed end of an athletic water bottle directly into the hole will avoid spillage and wetting the surface. The amount of water must be minimal, just enough to moisten the very gravel and bottom sand. The gravel layer acts as a reservoir.

The scorpions will dig to the depth they prefer. The number of straws is determined by the size of the cage. There is less chance of the scorpions digging them up if they are placed along the cage periphery. A fairly even gradient can be maintained in a large cage if a few straws are inserted away from the edges. Great care must be taken that the amount of moisture is minimal and maintained at a fairly constant but very low level.

Testing a Scorpion's Moisture Needs

Temporarily supply a larger cage than is necessary—twice the size is perfect. Prepare a 2-inch (5 cm) or deeper layer of three parts sand to one part clean, microwaved potting soil or mulch. Spread an equal number of pieces of bark or flat rocks on the surface of the cage. Lightly spray one-half of the surface with water several times to assure some has reached the lowest level. It should be slightly damp; under no circumstances soak the substrate. Some moisture will wick toward the dry side, providing a gradient. Increase the moisture content of the soil at one end while leaving the other end dryer. Do not forget to include a very shallow water dish somewhere toward the center.

Lightly mist the far end of the "wet side" every few days to assure it maintains a stable dew point. Over a period of weeks, the scorpion will have moved into a specific area that may be assumed to be its preferred moisture level. Frequent trips to the water dish are an excellent hint that moisture needs are high.

When judiciously used, the straw system works well with desert taxa. Misting may be needed for tropical or grassland forms. If several specimens are available, experiment with a variety of substrate mixtures as well. Continue the procedure. Within a week or so, the scorpion will have chosen its preferred environment. The scorpion should then be moved into a smaller cage that provides its optimum living conditions.

A scorpion's actions will provide additional clues to its needs. If it spends a great deal of time on its water dish, it probably needs a moister substrate or higher humidity. If it sits off the substrate on top of its furnishings, it probably needs to be dryer. Take notes as all of these observations are important and will be of interest to other keepers.

Hides

Anything with a flat side that when placed against the substrate will allow the scorpion to dig under it can be used as a hide. Depending upon the keeper's aesthetics, many small materials that are found around the house, and usually discarded, will suffice. The majority prefer to use rocks, bark, and other natural materials, because they are more attractive and readily available. Pet shops sell cork bark, the primary choice of all kinds of small animal keepers for many years.

Naturalistic clay and stone retreats that are specially designed for small reptiles and invertebrates are also available. However, they are expensive. Some have built-in water dishes.

Be certain to wash and rinse thoroughly everything you add to the cage to remove any residue it may be carrying, including soap. Placing the items into a microwave oven for a few minutes is an effective method of drying and sterilizing furnishings.

Flat rocks can be stacked and glued together with silicone aquarium cement to form safe crevices for flat-rock and other lithophilic scorpions. Be especially careful that the glue has fully cured and that all remnants of the solvent odor have evaporated. The flattened shape of a scorpion is a clue that it prefers tight spaces. It is more secure when in contact with the top and sides of its hiding place.

Clay tile: Small pieces of ceramic (clay) tile are widely available and are excellent hides. A visit to a garden center or floor tile company will provide a myriad of sizes and shapes befitting any size scorpion. Shards of clay flowerpots as well as those of almost any ceramic item work well, and they are usually given away if requested.

Vertical bark: Arboreal and climbing scorpions do best hiding in the spaces between vertically stacked pieces of bark. Because these scorpions are usually small and very quick, the container should be relatively tall and the bark should not reach all the way to the top. A few stands of stacked bark are excellent for communally kept scorpions. These stands help avoid conflicts by permitting each scorpion its own retreat and territory. Some of these species need a vertical slant to molt successfully.

Plastic containers and fixtures: Several different diameters and lengths of plastic plumbing fixtures (elbows, tees, end caps, and short pieces of pipe), partially buried into the substrate, make excellent tunnels and burrow entrances. Lightly sanding (with medium-grade sandpaper) the inside reduces the smooth texture, permitting a better foothold for the scorpions.

Peat moss pots: Garden shops carry inexpensive, lightweight seed starter pots made from compressed peat moss and compressed coconut husk fiber. When cut in half lengthwise, these make excellent retreats for most scorpions. They have a natural look, come in several sizes, and retain moisture very well, particularly when sprayed lightly each week. They are excellent moisture-retaining retreats for scorpions that are undergoing a molt. Vertically stacking strips cut from the pots make excellent hides for small climbing scorpions.

Halves or pieces of coconut shell offer a similar, natural, moisture-retaining retreat but are a bit more difficult to acquire. Pet suppliers sell them as hides for reptiles. They come with an inverted U-shaped entrance cut into one edge. A quick search of the Internet will reveal several suppliers. A few telephone calls to local oriental restaurants may turn up someone willing to save the shells for you.

Coconut fiber sheeting: Some pet suppliers sell thin sheets of compressed coconut husk fiber as moisture-retaining background for land crabs and similar animals. The same material is available from garden shops as liners for hanging baskets. It is an excellent all-around material for lining tropical scorpion cages or, when cut into small pieces, for use as surface or vertical hides. It absorbs moisture well when misted.

Temperature

Desert, subtropical, and tropical scorpions require warm temperatures, 80°–87°F (26.7°–30.6°C), to feed, digest, and grow normally. In contrast, those from temperate regions will do well at 70–78° F (21.1–25.6°C) or room temperature. If your scorpions need high temperatures, heating the entire room may be the best alternative. Hot air rises. So place scorpions that prefer slightly cooler temperatures close to the floor and those preferring warmer ones higher, toward the ceiling.

Keeping your scorpions in a large closet or cabinet is another way of controlling temperatures. Many auxiliary heat sources, with built-in thermostats, work well. Caution must be taken always to assure maximum safety when using any heating device.

Most scorpions, including those from hot, dry environments, should have a drop of approximately 10°F (1.2°C) to their nighttime temperature to emulate their natural day-to-night fluctuation. Tropical forms do well with a constantly warm temperature.

Advanced keepers take great pains to acclimatize scorpions carefully and to induce breeding by providing a seasonal change in ambient temperature, combined with changes in light cycles and humidity. They attempt to emulate a circadian rhythm (natural cycles to stimulate innate functions).

Heat Tapes

If the room cannot be easily heated, individual heat sources should be used. Many heating products designed for keeping reptiles are usable for arachnids as well. The best of these are the 3-inch (7.6 cm) and 10-inch (25.4 cm) wide, paper thin, plastic heat tapes. They are designed to spread heat over the entire surface, preventing one area from getting too hot. The narrower tapes work well with nearly all cages, whereas the wider ones are best suited for very large enclosures. They can be bought by the linear foot and cut to the desired length. Electrical connections are straightforward and simple but may require adult supervision to be completely safe. Some sources sell the tapes precut to your specifications and fully wired.

The tape should be affixed to the back wall of the shelf on which the cage is located. This position serves three functions. First, the tape remains outside the cage. Second, it is a precaution against overheating. Third, it enables the scorpion to move away from the heat source, seeking its own temperature gradient.

Thermometers

Plastic strip thermometers that stick onto an aquarium wall are an excellent method of monitoring a cage's temperature. They are so inexpensive that every cage should have one. Place it level with the substrate, near the warmest part of the cage. Sensitive, battery-operated, digital thermometers are available at electronics stores (such as Radio Shack). They can be read in degrees Fahrenheit and degrees Celsius, have a low and high memory, and record the temperature at their location. Most also have a remote-sensing probe.

Other versions have a thermometer and humidity gauge but no remote probe. Placing one inside a cage shows the temperature and

▬▬▬ CAUTION! ▬▬▬

Other Heating Devices

Radiant heat bulbs, hot rocks, and other in-cage heaters can become too hot. There is also the ever-present electric wire that must be brought into the cage. Many European keepers use a dangling red bulb of wattage proportionate to the size of the cage for heat. The red light minimally affects the scorpion's activities. Here again, however, is the electric cord problem. Advanced keepers with larger collections should investigate the wide variety of heating supplies and thermostats that are made for reptile hobbyists.

humidity accurately. These are particularly useful when calculating the amount of moisture needed to achieve constant humidity.

Cannibalism

Cannibalism is a way of life—or should I say way of death—for many scorpions. As aggressive predators, they see any small, moving creature as a meal and react accordingly—attack, kill, and eat! However, there are many situations when they do not attack.

Certain chemical and tactile sensors apparently block the initial attack reaction. A mother scorpion will rarely eat her newborns but may have no qualms about consuming the babies of others. She seems to identify her own by smell and touch.

Some species can live communally without eating conspecifics. However, if a member of another species enters the territory, it is just another food animal. In some situations, communal feeding may occur.

Most scorpions are solitary and frequently will attack and consume a scorpion that wanders by. A few are predominantly nomadic and cannibalistic, seeking out and eating any suitable invertebrate, including another scorpion. A starving scorpion will eat anything it can kill.

Communal Species

Why some scorpions can live rather tranquilly in communal groups while others are fierce adversaries is not known. There are still other groups that tolerate neighbors but maintain and protect territories. This likely has to do with the prevalence of food, limited proper habitat, and small home range. Some species are very aggressive predators of any scorpion.

Although a few keepers have been able to house different species together, regardless of how nonaggressive the species may be, doing so seems to be taunting fate. In the wild, a few different taxa are found living in close proximity. If you choose to try mixing species in a cage, food must be given to them at least once a week so that they are always adequately fed. A water dish should be available at least weekly. The scorpions should be all approximately the same size, and more than enough hiding places should be provided throughout the cage.

Cage size limits the range of a species, forcing the inhabitants to live within predetermined and human-induced boundaries. At times, this situation becomes stressful and cannibalism may occur. Females may live together for years,

but suddenly one will attack and kill another without obvious provocation.

The amount of surface area is usually the important factor in whether or not scorpions become cannibalistic. Arboreal scorpions (for example, many bark scorpions) can be kept communally in a tall cage with limited ground area, provided there are several vertical places affording numerous small cracks and crevices in which they can hide. A hollow section of palm tree trunk, curls of cork bark, or the basal sections of attached epiphytes are nearly perfect microhabitats. If you augment the vertical surface by covering the floor with a 3-inch (7.5 cm) layer of moistened cypress mulch, peat, or coconut husk, as many as ten adults will live amicably in a tall, 15-gallon (57 L) aquarium.

Widely known for its cannibalistic behavior, this 5th instar Smerigurus mesaensis *becomes a meal for an adult female of the same species.*

Several **Mesobuthus martensii** *can be safely kept together if they are well fed, the enclosure is sizable, and there are numerous hiding places.*

Commonly Available Communal Species

Dozens of gregarious ground dwellers, like emperor scorpions and forest scorpions, are frequently seen at pet shops heaped together in a 20-gallon (76 L) aquarium. Unfortunately, those conditions are terribly overcrowded. Four to six similarly sized specimens, preferably two or three pairs, are appropriate for a cage with that amount of floor area. The substrate should be at least 3 inches (7.6 cm) of a moist, tropical soil mixture. A half dozen pieces of cork bark 6–10 inches (15–25 cm) in length should be strewn about the surface as retreats. A large, shallow water dish completes the furnishings.

The Israeli gold scorpion (*Scorpio maurus palmatus*) is a small, communal desert species. Six (again preferably three pairs) can safely live (relatively safely) in a 10-gallon (38 L) aquarium. A layer of sandy desert mixture 3–5 inches (7.6–12.7 cm) thick is a good choice for a substrate. A few flat stones, pieces of weathered wood, or cork bark placed on the surface supply a variety of hiding places. Some prefer to make scrapes, so include flat objects large enough for them to make a space under. A water dish should be provided weekly.

Handling

As stated previously, there are no reasons for free-handling scorpions. However, at times, they must be moved or transported. The best, safest, and least-stressful method is scooping. An extra-large soup spoon (used for stirring large pots) is the perfect implement for catching all but the biggest scorpions. Scoop up the animal (including some substrate) with a quick, direct sweep, or very gently prod the animal into the spoon with a pencil, soda straw, small artist's paintbrush, or similar implement. Hold a container beneath the tool to catch the scorpion if it falls. Larger scorpions and those that are to be moved more than a few feet are best scooted into a plastic container and secured with a lid (like a deli cup).

An excellent tool for moving a small-to-medium scorpion is a small foam rubber paintbrush. The animal is gently prodded to walk onto the foam brush, which it will likely do fairly willingly. The scorpion's tarsi will grasp and hold fast to the roughly textured surface with minimal stress, allowing the animal to be moved easily. These brushes are widely available in craft, hobby, and the paint departments of home improvement stores.

A good escape preventive is to place the cage into a larger container, eliminating an immediate place of escape. Plastic sweater boxes can hold smaller cages, and a sink or bathtub is an excellent place for larger ones. Be sure to block the drain.

Forceps

In emergency situations and tight spaces, rubber-tipped forceps (oversized tweezers) are the tool of choice. A pair should always be kept within easy reach of your scorpions. Special, 6-, 8-, and 10-inch (15, 20, and 25 cm), rubber-tipped tweezers are available in some pet shops or by mail order. The elastic tips allow a firm grip on the smooth, hard surface of the exoskeleton and help prevent injury to the scorpion.

Great care should be exercised when handling a scorpion with forceps. Grip it by a metasomal segment, preferably by the segment directly before the telson, and quickly lift it upward, free of the substrate. The pressure should be just firm enough to hold the animal but not enough to injure it. There is a fine line here to prevent external or internal injury. Practice is needed to perfect the technique. Be prepared for the

scorpion to react by forcefully grabbing the forceps with its chelae. This is not a safe way of picking up robust species because their weight exerts a great amount of strain on their metasomas. Since this is so stressful for all scorpions, it is not the preferred method. However, it frequently is the only way to grab an escaping scorpion. Quickly placing an inverted small cup over the animal is a handy and safe way to stop a running scorpion. Sliding a thin piece of cardboard under the cup over the animal will simplify entrapping and transporting it.

More About Handling

Scorpions react violently to being grabbed. They twist and turn, grabbing and pulling with their chelae in an attempt to escape. Only midsize and large scorpions should be handled with forceps. Because of their diminutive size and obvious fragility, tiny, newborn, and recently molted scorpions should never be grabbed with forceps.

The safest, least stressful method of picking up a scorpion is shown here.

Ventilation is very important for keeping your scorpion healthy. Covering the entire top of a cage with a sheet of glass or plastic should not be done. Air and ventilation holes are a must. Even if high humidity is required, there should always be some air movement to eliminate stagnant air and prevent the development of bacteria and mold and to keep the scorpions healthy. The simplest way is to place vents at opposite ends of the cage.

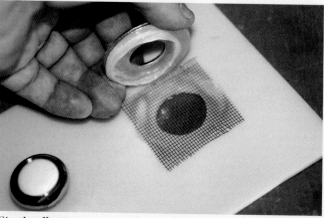

Simple, effective aquarium tops are relatively easy to make with a few tools and readily available materials.

Materials:
- *sheet acrylic cut to fit into the lip on the top of the aquarium*
- *aluminum or steel screen material (plastic is not sturdy enough) cut into 3-inch (7.6 cm) squares*
- *large, flat, steel washers with .75-inch (1.9 cm) hole*
- *drawer pull*
- *tube of strong all-purpose adhesive*
- *electric drill*
- *bit with 1 inch (2.5 cm)*
- *bit to suit screw on drawer pull*
- *matte knife*

One vent hole drilled at each end of the acrylic (equidistant from the end and edge) should be adequate for aquariums of 10 gallons (4.5 L) or smaller. The number of holes should double when the aquarium size is doubled [e.g., 20 gallons (9 L), 4 holes]. Glue screen patch covering the hole and glue washer over the screening giving a neat appearance. When dry, the seeped glue and excess screen are trimmed with the matte knife. A hole to affix the drawer pull is drilled in the center of the acrylic to facilitate removing the lid.

Air and Ventilation

If plastic containers are used, drilling or burning holes into the sides or top solves the problem. An inexpensive soldering pen with a fine point (available at hobby or craft stores) is the nearly perfect tool for quickly making three or four holes in dozens of containers. Care must be taken that the orifices are small enough to prevent escapes. This is especially important if the scorpion gives birth. Many newborns are extremely small. By making the holes in the sides of the containers, slightly below the top, the containers can be stacked. This efficiently uses shelf space while permitting airflow.

Larger plastic containers, such as shoe boxes and sweater boxes, are best with bigger air holes drilled into the plastic and covered with aluminum screening. They should be no larger than 1 inch (2.5 cm) in diameter. One hole should be drilled in the back, above the surface of the substrate, and another on the top at the opposite end. This will allow cross-ventilation. If the containers are stacked, the top hole will be obstructed, so a matching large hole should be made in the side across the container from it. Drilling or burning several smaller holes provides adequate ventilation, but larger ones are better. Larger vents are compulsory to maintain a dry desert environment.

Most aquariums produced today are all glass with a molded plastic top and bottom frame for appearance and rigidity and to prevent the corners from chipping. There is a small lip on the inside edge of the top plastic frame that is meant to hold a glass cover but is also perfect for holding a homemade, fit-in top.

There are two designs for easy-to-build, fit-in tops: aluminum window screens and a modified sheet of acrylic/plastic. Many variations are possible by combining the two concepts. With some thought, you will likely produce a style that best suits your particular need.

A Screen Top

By using a few simple tools and preformed parts, you can fabricate aluminum window screen covers quite simply. The materials (aluminum screening, aluminum frame rails, plastic corner pieces, and soft plastic beading) are relatively inexpensive and available in hardware and do-it-yourself stores.

1. Measure the dimension on the inside lip of the plastic aquarium top. Remember to account for the size of the plastic corners. Cut the side rails with a hacksaw or small handsaw.

2. Snap the rails together with corner pieces, and you will have a square and rigid frame.

3. Cut the aluminum screening with a sharp knife or scissors and press in place. Secure it with the special plastic beading by using a pizza cutter-like tool made specifically for the job.

4. Trim the excess, and the top is finished.

A one-piece screen top is most suitable for desert cages because it does not retain moisture well.

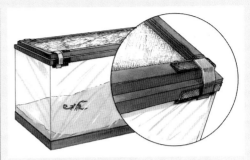

The screened cage top with Velcro closure (shown in inset).

An Acrylic/Plastic Top

Acrylic/plastic tops are simple to construct, less expensive, and efficient. For aquariums up to 10 gallons (38 L), two sheets of 0.17-inch (3 mm) plastic material should be cut to fit the inside lip of the top snuggly. Using a fine-toothed saw or very sharp matte knife will insure a clean edge. Temporarily tape the two sheets together along the edges.

FOOD AND FEEDING

When compared with the way other animals eat, scorpions are bizarre. When viewed close up, their feeding habits are the stuff that makes science fiction creatures gory and terrifying. Food is predigested before it is sucked into the body. As unusual as it seems, predigestion is not unique to scorpions; most arthropods also do it.

The Mechanics of Feeding

Prey is grabbed by the chelae and brought to the chelicerae, where it is consumed. The food animal may be killed or eaten alive, depending on how much it struggles. The chelicerae, which resemble and function like small scissors, have cutting surfaces that tear and grind the prey animal into minute pieces and then pass the pastelike food into the preoral cavity.

The food paste is mixed with digestive juices in the preoral cavity and strained by a pair of maxillary brushes (each is an oval-shaped grouping of tiny, rigid bristles) to remove indigestible parts. Brushes contain chemoreceptors that have an unknown function. However, these chemoreceptors likely discern different chemicals, thereby providing a primitive form of tasting. In addition, they are used to groom

Here **Pandinus carimanus,** *one of the larger scorpions widely available in pet shops, feasts on a roach.*

and clean the pedipalps and legs. Matted debris is discharged, while the liquefied food is sucked into the gut.

Further digestion and absorption take place in the gut. The mesosoma can distend noticeably, enabling a massive intake of food. Nutrients are slowly digested and absorbed over a period of days. How quickly this occurs depends on the ambient temperature. Higher temperatures expedite the process. Feces, an almost dry, chalky, white substance containing mostly guanine and uric acid, are passed from the anus located at the distal end of the metasoma immediately before the telson.

Feeding Strategies

Scorpions are opportunistic predators that employ two fundamental strategies to procure food: ambushing and foraging. Each has its benefits and drawbacks.

Voracious feeding is typical of **Heterometrus longimanus**, *here shown eating one giant mealworm while crushing another in its chela.*

Ambushing: Fossorial scorpions spend most of their lives within or near their burrows and are ambush predators. They move up to the hidden entrances of their burrows at dusk. Then they sit and wait with their chelae open, poised, ready to snare any luckless passing meal. Most ambush predators crush their prey and use venom sparingly, if at all. Food may be consumed where it is captured or taken into the burrow and eaten. Ambush predation is efficient, expending very little energy. Also, because the burrow is readily available for escape, ambushing is a relatively safe hunting strategy, preventing the scorpions from becoming the prey of other carnivores.

Foraging is extremely different than ambushing. A forager's tactics expend considerable energy. Because these scorpions leave the protection of their hiding places and actively search for food, they face more inherent risks than those that ambush. Foragers are smaller, are quicker, climb more freely, and have fairly potent venom. Because they are on the move so much, they may encounter other scorpions, which they will eat or possibly be eaten by. The giant sand scorpion, *Smeringurus mesaensis*, of the southwestern United States is known for its cannibalistic tendencies. Most of its diet consists of other scorpions, including those of its own species.

At least one devil scorpion—*Tityus fasciolatus*, another South American scorpion genus—*Armitermes*, and the Asian *Chaerilus* live in termite mounds. The proximity of such a large food source makes procuring food very simple. The scorpions move around within the mound, stop at a likely spot, and pick off termites as they walk by. As long as the mound remains viable, a colony of scorpions could live and reproduce for generations without having to leave its confines.

A Balanced Diet

A hungry scorpion will eat almost anything small enough for it to grab and kill. However, there seems to be a high-end and a low-end size preference. Logically, larger scorpions eat larger food items than do smaller ones. In fact, bigger scorpions have trouble catching small prey. Scorpions with large chelae are well adapted to subdue and hold large prey. The favored prey size for most species, however, appears to be one-third that of the scorpion. It is unusual for a scorpion to take a food animal more than two-thirds its

Opistophthalmus ecristatus waits at its burrow's entrance for a meal to pass within range.

body size; half or slightly less is usually the upper limit. In fact, many scorpions will run away from prey that is too large. During times when prey is abundant, insects with thick, hard exoskeletons and those that produce repugnant chemicals are commonly refused. For example, few scorpions eat wood lice.

Crickets are the main choice for captive scorpions. They are available from many sources, inexpensive, and easy to rear and maintain. With few exceptions, they are excellent food animals for nearly all scorpions. The scorpion's low metabolism (allowing low energy consumption) and the ability to consume large meals enable it to fast for long periods.

Feast or famine feeding combined with seasonal changes in temperature and humidity, which necessitate periods of prolonged rest (hibernation and aestivation), are relevant for a scorpion's long-term survival. Also, regulating food intake of captive specimens assures that there are lean periods that prevent the unhealthy equivalent of obesity. These strategies (emulating circadian rhythms) should be employed as part of captive husbandry to ensure a healthy animal.

Some Less-Desirable Food Animals

Most pest insects, such as ants, termites, and cockroaches, can be used. However, they may have potential drawbacks. In addition, the thought of rearing them is, well, gross! Their social habits, size, and potential for causing unwanted infestations make them problematical food animals. Certain social insects, bees in particular, have been used as food. Commercially available wax worms, *Galleria mellonella*, are fed to many kinds of insect-eating animals, but many scorpions refuse them. Also, they are extremely soft bodied and tend to ooze freely while being killed and eaten, leaving a sticky mess that may attract dangerous mites.

When and How Much Food

A fallacy that has been circulated for years is that if you feed a scorpion as much as it will eat, it will continue to eat, gorging itself to death. A hungry scorpion can eat a tremendous amount of food for its size, so much so that it will indeed gorge itself until its mesosoma is so swollen that it appears as though it will burst. However, when sated, it will stop and go into hiding to digest. If kept at its optimum temperature, the scorpion will digest this meal, defecate, and in a few days to a week, feed again. Alternatively, it may refuse to eat for some

time, perhaps several months. Healthy adult males are notorious for undertaking long fasts.

The amount of food given per feeding is arbitrary. However, it should be monitored and guided by concern for the animal's welfare. The quantity depends on the physical condition of the scorpion, the temperature at which it is being kept, and its age. A healthy scorpion will have good body weight and will not appear either gaunt or pudgy. Higher temperatures cause rapid metabolism, which requires additional food for the scorpion to maintain its weight.

Because they are growing constantly, young scorpions will eat as much as they can, frequently to the point of being gluttonous. They should be well fed, perhaps a few small food animals every three days, but not to the point of being continuously bloated.

Types of Food

In addition to crickets (see "HOW-TO: Rear Crickets as Food Items" at the end of this chapter), scorpions can subsist on a diet of various other insects.

Mealworms (*Tenebrio molitor*): Mealworms, the larvae of a species of darkling beetle, are an old standby food. They vary in size from 0.25–0.75 inches (6.4–10 mm) in length. Millions are raised as food for amphibians, lizards, birds, and small mammals. They are widely available at pet and bait shops.

Mealworms are easy to rear. Every scorpion keeper should have a colony or two as a backup food supply. They can be a godsend in winter months when crickets are difficult to acquire. Plastic sweater boxes make excellent rearing

The oversized chelae of **Opistacanthus asper** *easily hold this large cricket.*

Heterometrus fulvipes, *exported from the moist regions of India.*

containers because mealworms and the adult beetles do not climb well. Bran is the food of choice, but oats and other cereal grains will work.

Setting up a culture is very simple. Dump a few dozen of the larvae (or pupae if available) into a container with 3 inches (7.4 cm) of bran. Then add a piece of raw potato, carrot, squash, apple (sliced in half lengthwise), or cabbage leaf for moisture. Cover it with a few layers of newspaper or paper towel, and put it aside in a warm, dark spot. Replace the moist food source when it dries or is consumed. The container needs to be covered because the overall humidity will be so low that the food moisture will evaporate very quickly. The cover should have holes to allow adequate ventilation. When kept at room temperature, the mealworms will metamorphose into beetles. The adults will then lay eggs, starting a new cycle. All phases should be seen in a month or two, and then you can start to harvest.

The mealworms (larvae) will gather in the paper or can be sifted from the bran with a small, kitchen strainer. Any size mealworm can be used as food for your scorpions. Scorpions rarely eat the pupae (because they do not move) or adults. Instead, leave them to renew the colony. Every six months, sift the grain, discard the dry, powdery feces that have collected on the bottom, and place the remaining animals into fresh bran. A paper painter's mask should be worn when sifting to prevent inhaling the dry dust. Raw bran can be bought in health food stores by the pound or in feed stores in larger quantities. If more than a few dozen adults are in a culture, they should be discarded or used to start new cultures. They will eat their eggs if the container is too crowded.

Super mealworms (*Zoophobas morio*): The larvae of another darkling beetle, super mealworms, are available. They are several times larger than the larvae of regular mealworms, 1.5–2 inches (3.8–5.1 cm), and bulkier. These robust larvae of a tropical beetle have strong chewing mouthparts. They are capable of inflicting painful, possibly damaging, bites on small amphibians and lizards. They are no threat to midsize and larger scorpions since the scorpions make quick work in killing them. They eat rotting wood and sawdust and will chew their way out of light plastic deli cups.

Super mealworms are not cold tolerant and are more difficult and time-consuming to breed than regular mealworms. Nearly all that I have seen for sale are full-sized larvae, and they are much cheaper if purchased in large quantities. They can be kept as healthy larvae for up to two months in a plastic tub containing sawdust and held at a temperature of 60°–70°F (15.6°–21.1°C). They will perish at 50°F (10°C) or lower and will metamorphose if kept at a higher temperature.

Fruit flies (*Drosophila* spp.): Wingless and vestigial-winged fruit flies are tiny, mutant forms of normally winged flies. They are cultured for use in genetics experiments and as live tropical fish food. Their small size (0.15 inches/3.2 mm) makes them an excellent food for early instar and very small scorpions. Two species, *D. melanogaster* and the slightly larger *D. hydei*, are obtainable from mail-order biological supply houses and a number of professional *Drosophila* breeders. It is best to start by buying a complete rearing kit that includes bottles, sponge stoppers, culture medium, starter flies, and instructions. Although near perfect size, *D. hydei* readily climb and spend most of their time on the underside of the scorpion container's lid, out of the reach of most scorpions.

Roaches: Recently, several genera and species of roaches have become available as arachnid food. Some are strictly terrestrial and are claimed not to climb. The orange-spotted roach (*Blaptica dubia*) is highly touted for this trait and is said to be very hardy and not fly. Three common roaches, the German cockroach (*Blatella germanica*), the American cockroach (*Periplaneta americana*), and the Oriental cock-roach (*B. orientalis*), are eaten by some larger scorpions. Roaches have a distinct odor. Unlike tarantulas, many scorpions refuse them. Even though the Madagascan giant hissing roaches (*Gromphadorhina portentosa*) are widely available as pets, adults are huge, much too large for most scorpions. However, if the scorpions will eat them, immature animals are an excellent source of nutrients.

One taxon, *Blaberus craniiferus*, is available from time to time from scientific suppliers but is difficult to find. They cannot fly and are poor climbers. At least they cannot climb clean glass as readily as other roaches, so they can be kept in an aquarium. Take extra care that any container for roaches has no cracks or holes and has a very tight-fitting cover.

Because they are nocturnal, a red light source should be used for heat. Aside from almost any dry foodstuff, scrap vegetable matter is nutritious while supplying water. Some roaches can climb almost anything, so greater care must be taken to contain them. Because they will not walk through petroleum jelly, applying a thin band around the container, slightly below the top, will help keep them in. A band of vegetable cooking spray (for example, Pam) is equally effective.

Roaches are easy to breed; some think too easy. They can be kept basically the same way as crickets. Although debatable, the parasites and bacteria carried in the guts of wild-caught roaches could be harmful to the animals that prey upon them.

Fly maggots (*Musca spp.*): Fly larvae (maggots) are another food source for small- and medium-sized scorpions. They reproduce readily, frequently, and prodigiously during the warmer seasons. Several species are almost always lurking around. Simply leave a small piece of moist meat

Here a luckless Sphaerodactylid gecko is consumed by an adult **Pandinus cavimanus.**

outside in a wide-mouthed jar to spoil for a few days. Flies will find it and lay eggs. Small chunks of raw kidney or liver work well. Keep the meat moistened. In a few more days, the eggs will hatch and the meat will be alive with a writhing mass of maggots. If nurtured in a warm place, they will grow rapidly. Ground beef is not a good medium because it dries out rather than rotting.

Exposed meat is frequently infested with the smaller larva of blowflies and flesh flies first. Because of their size, they are less desirable as food items. When they first appear, place the meat into a small aquarium fishnet and rinse it with running water to wash them away.

Once the larger maggots appear, they should be fed to the scorpions in short order because they will metamorphose into adults in less than two weeks. Keeping them in a covered, ventilated container in the least-cold section of a refrigerator will slow down metamorphosis.

Termites are an excellent food source for the smallest scorpions but carry with them a potential of becoming a highly undesirable infestation. Almost any forest or trash pile will have rotting wood and logs harboring colonies of termites. There are several taxa, and all are good food sources.

The safest, as not being a threat to eat your home (literally), are rottenwood or dampwood termites, *Zootermopsis* spp. of the family Hodotermitidae. They live in all kinds of wood that are buried in the ground and subjected to extreme moisture and rotting. They are larger than the subterranean termites of the family Rhinotermitidae, the scourge of every homeowner.

A large colony of termites can be contained in a securely screen-covered aquarium, while a small colony will do well in a wide-mouthed plastic gallon jar or other container. Keep them in the wood in which they were collected. The wood must be kept moist; termites die from dehydration very quickly. Place the container into the dark at room temperature. By placing the wood on an overturned dinner plate that has been submerged in water (making an island) and keeping it that way, the termites will remain intact, eating the pulp and not crossing the water. They are harvested by pulling away small sections of the wood and shaking them into a plastic container.

If you keep only a few scorpions, the effort and time required to raise many kinds of food are probably not well spent. In such a case, it is more reasonable to buy crickets. Pet shops and bait stores are good local sources. Read the advertisements in reptile, aquarium, or fishing magazines for other food animal sources.

Almost any wooded lot will provide an adequate assortment of edible insects, such as grubs, beetles, grasshoppers, crickets, butterflies, and moths, throughout the warmer months. Be aware, however, that urban populations may be carrying a high pesticide and chemical load. When maintaining live foods, good housekeeping and cleanliness are paramount. Excess moisture can be a problem because it promotes mold growth and mites.

Adequate ventilation helps reduce the moisture problem.

House Crickets
(*Acheta domestica*)

Because of their diet, crickets contain a wide variety of vitamins, proteins, and minerals. Crickets should be healthy, well fed, and given water before using them as food. Gut loading (adding calcium to food animals) is unnecessary because its nutritive value for arachnids is thought to be nil.

Crickets can be purchased in many sizes ranging from newborn (pinheads) to adults. To save money, buy a quantity and raise them toward adulthood (1,000 small crickets cost about $25, including shipping). They grow at slightly different rates, so a variety of sizes are available at any given time. Pinheads take six weeks to

reach adulthood, and adults live approximately two to three weeks.

If you can allot the space, accept some odor, handle the chirping, and will spend a few hours a month maintaining them, crickets are simple to breed and extremely prolific. Aside from food, two things are required: a constant supply of clean water and a heat source. Sexing crickets is simple. Adult males chirp, and females have long median ovipositors.

A very large, deep, smooth-sided container is necessary to maintain a thriving colony. Two or three containers started at different times provide a continuous supply of all sizes. The simplest container is a plastic storage bin. It must be at least 16 inches (41 cm) deep to prevent the crickets from jumping out. Aside from keeping the crickets from escaping, a screened top permits excellent air circulation.

Add 0.5–.75 inches (1.3–1.9 mm) of clean, dry peat or sand and egg cartons or cardboard tubes from paper towels or toilet paper for hiding places. When crowded, crickets will become stressed and cannibalistic or may suffocate each other.

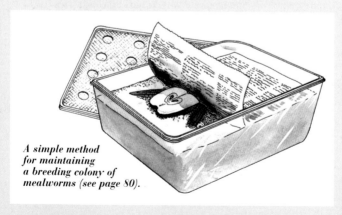

A simple method for maintaining a breeding colony of mealworms (see page 80).

AS FOOD ITEMS

Specially formulated cricket food is available, but small quantities are costly. Many kinds of crushed dry dog, cat, rodent, or other pet foods are good choices as cricket food. Some experimentation with different brands may be necessary since crickets may be discriminating in their choices. Basic inexpensive varieties, without flavoring, should be chosen.

Unmedicated chicken-laying mash is an excellent, inexpensive food. Be certain it is not medicated. The medicinal additives will destroy the natural flora in the crickets' guts, disturb the digestive balance, and likely kill them.

Scrap fruits and vegetables can be offered for nutritional and water content. Crickets dehydrate rapidly. As a consequence, a water reservoir, available from pet stores and mail-order cricket suppliers, must be accessible and filled with clean water at all times. Water-retaining crystals are a clean, safe way of providing water. A safely installed dangling spotlight bulb, of a size that will produce enough heat to maintain a temperature near 85°F (29.4°C), is needed for optimum production.

When properly cared for, crickets reproduce readily. Place a plastic container at least 6 inches (15.2 cm) in diameter with 1 inch (2.5 cm) of clean, damp (not soaking) sand or vermiculite in with adult crickets. The crickets will start to lay eggs almost immediately. If the substrate container is slightly sloped, excess moisture will drain toward the lower end.

Remove the container after a day or two. Place it inside a covered plastic sweater box with a fine layer of dry sand covering the bottom. Keep the container warm, ideally at 85°F (29.4°C). Check the dampness of the sand in the egg-bearing container every few days, and mist it lightly if it is drying conspicuously. It

A container for keeping crickets. Note the screened ventilation holes in the top.

should not be noticeably wet, just damp. In two weeks, hundreds of pinhead crickets will emerge. They can be fed the finely mashed food used for adults. A water dish, with gravel protruding above the surface, will provide water and avert drowning.

As the crickets grow, move them into a large container. In about six weeks, they will reach adulthood and the cycle will start over again. Change the substrate every month. The money saved and the constant availability of a variety of sizes of crickets is well worth the effort if you maintain a large scorpion collection.

One hazard of escaped crickets is their destructive appetite. Like their close relatives the roaches, they will find their way into and eat paper and cardboard containers of dry foods and bread. They will chew into fruits and show a distinct taste for the starch in the glue of book bindings. They will die for need of water.

BREEDING SCORPIONS

Most scorpion births in captivity are from females that have been inseminated in the wild before being captured. Few have been captive bred, but that is changing rapidly.

Captive Breeding

As with any species taken from the wild, a captive-breeding project should be undertaken to produce a viable supply for the future.

Reproduction in nature is cyclic, controlled by interrelated environmental factors, including weather, temperature, humidity, and probably photoperiods. The stimuli are so instinctive and complex that they may be all but impossible to duplicate in captivity.

Determining Males and Females

As basic as it seems, being certain that you have an adult sexual pair is paramount. Adults have fully developed reproductive systems and are able to breed. Subadults cannot mate but may have obvious secondary sexual character-

This female **Centruroides sculpturatus** *is burdened with approximately thirty 2nd instar young.*

istics. Determining the sex of certain taxa is relatively simple. With others, some experience and careful observation are required.

Body size: Generally, adult males are smaller and less bulky than females. This is particularly apparent in *Pandinus* and *Heterometrus* species. In many species, the segments of a male's metasoma are more elongated than the female's, making it noticeably longer. There is a very perceptible difference in the metasoma length of *Hadogenes* and many *Centruroides*.

Chelae: The size, massiveness, and amount of granulation are commonly greater on the chelae of males, particularly *Pandinus, Heterometrus,* and *Opistophthalmus* species. Pedipalps of some male scorpions are thinner and longer than the female's. In others, though, only the chelae are elongated, as in *Centruroides* and *Heterometrus*. It may not be as obvious, but males of the majority of forms have more prominent granulation over the surface of their exoskeletons.

A narrow chela distinguishes the female
Babycurus jacksoni *(left) from the*
male (right).

Some have prominent protrusions on their pedipalps and metasomas. However, this is not true in *Tityus* and *Centruroides* species.

The comblike pectines offer a good, quick-to-recognize secondary sexual characteristic. In the majority of taxa, males have longer pectines that frequently curve slightly and possess a higher number of "teeth" than females. The safest way to check pectines is to place the scorpion into a shallow, clear plastic container with a paper towel or sponge applying some pressure from above. Turn the container upside down, and start counting "teeth." A plastic, disposable petri dish is an excellent choice, and clear plastic sandwich bags will work.

An almost foolproof method is to look closely at the genital operculum. It will require careful scrutiny and possibly the use of a magnifying glass to be sure. Males of most species have a pair of tiny protrusions (genital papillae) at the rear of the genital operculum.

A "Romantic" Atmosphere

Tropical scorpions may mate more than once a year. For others, mating is a seasonal activity, mostly initiated by climate and weather. In regions where there is a change of seasons (including desert areas), scorpions cease feeding at the advent of winter and retire to a shelter, remaining dormant until the temperature rises.

Possible mating stimulus: Rainfall is generally associated with springtime and may be the stimulus for mating. In arid regions, during long, hot, dry spells, scorpions go into a dormant stage, estivation. Prey is much scarcer until the summer rains start. Altering these climatic conditions in captivity has been successful in sexually arousing reptiles and amphibians.

Caging: Unless they are a communal species, the potential breeders should be caged separately before attempting a mating, and they should be well fed and healthy.

Female scorpions should be well established in their cages, with satisfactory substrate, hiding places, and a smooth flat rock at least twice the size of the female. Do not completely clean and refurbish the cage within a month of cooling or before attempting to breed them, because the scorpions must not undergo the stress.

Cooling: Although not necessary with some taxa, a cooling period of a month or two during the winter seems to be a good idea.

Other Stimuli: Also, it appears to be beneficial not to feed them, to keep them away from light, and to avoid disturbing them. Scorpions are sensitive to vibrations, and this may be more of a factor than has been realized. The drop in temperature should not be extreme, between 15°–20°F (8.3–11°C) lower than the normal temperature. As a precaution against dehydrating, a shallow dish of water should be available. Alternatively, a light, periodic misting should be done to cages of all but those scorpions from very arid environments.

Bring the environment back to its usual state. Wait a week or two for the scorpions to acclimate, and offer food. The females will be ravenous. The males may not feed, will likely be unsettled, and will wander about their cages. This is a sign that they are preparing to find a mate. Continue feeding as much as they will eat for a few weeks, until they are fat and healthy.

In the second week, mist the cage (not the scorpions directly) light to moderately, once a day for a few days. Mist just enough to moisten the surface and raise the humidity but not cause saturation and flooding. Take care when misting the cages of desert scorpions. They may become stressed or actually drown if partially submerged.

Some desert scorpions may be stimulated to breed by having the temperature elevated to near 95°F (35°C) for a few weeks during the summer months and lightly misting the cage a few times at the end of this period. This would coincide with the advent of their normal rainy season.

Making Certain One Will Not Be the Other's Lunch

It is time to introduce the male into the cage. He should be placed into a small container and released as far away from her and from her hide as possible. Do this gingerly to prevent stressing either animal. Observe them in the lowest light level possible to be sure neither attacks the other. It is not uncommon for one of the mates (usually the male) to be killed and eaten, sometimes after mating.

The following is a typical mating sequence, although courtship varies greatly from family to family and from species to species.

In a few minutes, the male begins to explore his new surroundings and sense the female's presence. Some (perhaps all) females emit sex

The telson of the female **Hadogenes paucidens** *(above) is much shorter than that of the male (below).*

pheromones (volatile chemical substances) that inform the male that she is nearby and receptive. He begins vibrating, rapidly moving his legs and shaking his body, sending vibrations through the substrate.

The female recognizes his presence through these vibrations and leaves her hiding place to rush at him in a mock attack, sometimes striking with her metasoma, her telson safely tucked underneath. They move apart, and a series of additional mock attacks are initiated. The male may sting an intersegmental membrane of the female's body, leaving the aculeus imbedded for as long as 20 minutes. If venom is injected, it likely anesthetizes and calms her, preventing normal aggressive, cannibalistic tendencies.

While facing each other, he grabs her pedipalps with his, and they dance about. This *promenade à deux* continues (usually lasting five

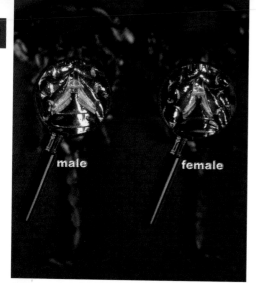

The longer, more numerous, comblike prominences of the Heterometrus spinifer on the left distinguish the male from the female on the right.

minutes to an hour) until the male, while using his pectines, finds a suitable surface on which to place his spermatophore, such as a flat rock. He deposits the stalked, freestanding spermatophore from his genital operculum and maneuvers her over it. She lowers her forebody toward him, squats, and forces the spermatophore into her operculum. Pressure caused by her moving backward releases the sperm into her reproductive tract. He pacifies her by grabbing and rubbing her chelicerae with his. The "kiss" continues for the brief, quiet period when she is taking in the spermatophore.

Immediately, the pair unclasps. The female remains over the spermatophore stalk for a few seconds, swaying back and forth. Material from the spermatophore plugs the opening of her operculum, preventing other males from being able to inseminate her. The male attempts a hasty retreat, to prevent becoming a meal. However, nearly a third of the time, males fail

in this endeavor. If the male survives the mating, remove him immediately. In the wild, some males may mate as many as a dozen times in a season, with several females. The time needed to produce a new spermatophore is not known, but only one is present for a mating.

Mating in a Communal Cage

Although it can be initiated, mating in a communal cage is usually a spontaneous event. Starting at dusk, there will be noticeable activity in communal cages, with males pursuing females and possibly sparring with other males. If the males are fighting, their chelae will be folded back and they will be pushing each other, like miniature earth-moving equipment. When mating, the chelae are used to pull and clasp each other. With the room lights out, the entire proceedings can be observed with UV light. This may give you the opportunity to rescue the occasional male that might be killed by an overly aggressive cage mate. Smaller males are more likely to be harassed and injured by larger ones. Regardless, the scorpion mating ritual is a complex, fascinating act of nature to watch.

When a Male Is Simply Not Needed

In some species, viable sperm from one mating can be retained within a female for quite some time. Some buthids may produce as many as four litters without remating. The number of litters produced from one mating is not known for some families, but is known for others. This explains why captive females seem to become pregnant spontaneously when no males are present. It is fairly common for recently captured females to be pregnant or carrying sperm.

Parthenogenesis: Some scorpions reproduce without males, by parthenogenesis, an unusual form of reproduction where offspring are produced without the need for sperm to fertilize the egg. One species of devil scorpion, *Tityus serratus*, and some Asian populations of a widely distributed scorpion, *Liocheles australasiae*, have reproduced parthenogenically. Not uncommon in insects, it is rare in arachnids.

Pregnancy

Gestation may take from 2 to 18 months, with little visible sign of anything happening for most of that time. The female should be maintained normally. To promote adequate growth of the embryos, the cage should be kept at the warmer end of its range and the female fed more than adequately. Underfed, pregnant females commonly absorb some or all of their embryos.

During the last month or so of gestation, the female's mesosoma will expand noticeably, giving the appearance of having eaten a huge meal. The intersegmental membranes will be stretched to their limits. Frequently, dozens of miniature, white scorpions will be visible within her. She will reduce food intake and may refuse to feed completely. It is wise to remove pregnant females from community cages because larger scorpions will eat a great number of early instars.

Fresh water should always be available. The pregnant Scorpion's temperament will probably turn aggressive. She will become more reclusive, possibly not venturing out of hiding at all. Do not disturb her in any way. Stress may cause her to absorb the embryos.

*Bulging sides reveal this **Odonturus dentatus** to be gravid and soon to give birth.*

Birth

In a week or so, the female will surface with a few to perhaps a hundred (depending on the taxon) small, chunky, white, newborn scorpions covering her back. All scorpions give birth to living young instead of laying eggs. Parturition may take a few hours to a few days to complete. Larger scorpions tend to have fewer and larger young, while smaller species may have a great number of tiny ones. As each newborn passes through the genital aperture, the mother helps it with her front feet. The newborns immediately climb the mother's legs and onto her back, where they ride for several days, until their first molt.

Stress must be kept at a minimum or mother scorpions may eat their young. Feed as much as she will eat to restore the nutrients used in producing the young. She may drink a lot of water. Be certain to remove uneaten live crickets that will eat young scorpions.

The small size of an adult **Diplocentrus peloncillensis** *is evidenced by this ballpoint pen.*

Scorpions from temperate regions usually give birth in the spring or fall. Tropical forms may give birth during any season.

Raising Instars

Newborn scorpions do not need food for a week or so, living off of stored nutrients until after their first molt. However, before their first molt they are susceptible to desiccation and will frequently die if taken from their mother's back, believed to be important for providing a regulated moisture gradient.

Mother's Protection of Newborns

Because newborn scorpions are helpless and vulnerable for the first ten days of their lives, their mother's protection is preeminent to their survival. She may aggressively chase or kill other scorpions that get too near.

A few days after molting, the young begin to darken as their exoskeleton hardens. They leave their mother periodically and begin to look for food. When frightened, they scurry back to her for protection. In a few more days, they begin to fend for themselves. Mother emperor scorpions may show continued maternalism—they feed their young. By killing, crushing, and tearing open prey that is too big for the babies, she enables them to feed on the softer inner tissues. Other mother scorpions are said to demonstrate similar behavior.

Things to Be Aware Of

Young of many tropical scorpions need high humidity and temperatures to feed, grow, and molt without problems. Emperor scorpion babies thrive in moist environments, with nearly 100% humidity and temperatures of 90–100°F (32.2–37.8°C). Immature forest scorpions prefer similar conditions. It is a good idea to mist a portion of the cages of most scorpions that have young.

Instar bark scorpions, devil scorpions, and other arboreal forms frequently suffer fatality from not molting properly. Include vertical climbs and hides in their cages and mist them periodically.

Giant hairy scorpions and other obligate burrowing mother scorpions are highly cannibalistic. If stressed or if conditions are not just right, she simply eats her young. It may be that birthing normally takes place within her burrow and the babies do not leave until they have molted and are ready to feed for themselves. If you are fortunate to have them molt successfully into their second instar, they should be immediately separated from their mother. Additionally, because the young are highly cannibalistic, they should be placed into individual containers.

Few keepers have been able to raise hairy scorpion young beyond the first few instars. These scorpions have trouble molting completely. Apparently, their environmental and dietary needs are not being met. The problem seems to be humidity related. However, the type of soil they require for burrowing into or some other unknown variable may instead be the cause.

Feeding the Little Guys

The biggest problem with raising early-instar scorpions is providing prey small enough for them to eat. Those of the larger taxa such as *Pandinus*, *Heterometrus*, and *Hadogenes* are big enough to eat small crickets. However, the majority of other scorpion instars are too small. Some will eat freshly killed larger insects that have been crushed to expose the moist inner tissues. Unfortunately, most will require an almost constant supply of minute insects.

Purchasing food items: Pinhead crickets can be purchased at some pet shops and are a nearly perfect food animal for very small scorpions. Wingless fruit flies (*Drosophila*) are an excellent, easy-to-raise food source, but are difficult to purchase anywhere except from mail-order sup-

———— T I P ————

What Is an Instar?

Instars are the times in an arachnid's life between molts. They are sequentially numbered. The last one is when sexual maturity (adulthood) is attained.

pliers. The best way of having small food animals available is to raise your own fruit flies, which require reculturing every 2 or 3 weeks.

Cannibalizing: One method is to allow the immature scorpions to cannibalize each other until a manageable number of the healthiest is obtained. As cruel as this first appears, it is a common happenstance in nature. Some species have dozens of babies, many of which may not be strong or healthy enough to survive. It permits keepers to devote their energy and resources on raising the healthiest animals available. Regardless of the amount of care given to rearing young, most will not grow to adulthood. As few as 1 percent of immature specimens survive to adulthood in the wild.

Of great importance: Maintaining proper humidity is a serious variable when trying to raise immature scorpions. Many taxa are prone to desiccate very rapidly. The availability of some moisture appears to aid molting. A very shallow dish of water (a plastic bottle cap containing some gravel) should be provided at all times. Gel water is the best way to offer them water so they will not drown. Free water is extremely dangerous to very small species. Capillary action from the water surface can hold them, covering their spiracles and drowning them.

SCORPION HEALTH

Several considerations influence a scorpion's normal development and subsequent maturity. To keep scorpions successfully, you must provide the parts of their natural history that are most important to them. As we have seen, scorpions actually require very little compared with most animals.

Normal Development

Scorpions will grow faster if they are fed frequently and kept at higher temperatures. However, rapid growth is not necessarily a valued asset. Normal development of all the organs of their bodies, so that they are capable of functioning appropriately, must be the primary consideration of scorpion keeping. As stated previously, seasonal changes in climate and temperature are sound husbandry practices.

A Cooling Period

As discussed in the chapter on breeding, a cooling period of one to two months has been suggested to initiate reproduction. A slight drop in evening temperatures will also help adjust the daily cycle. Another consideration is shortening the daylight portion of the daily light cycle to correspond with the cooler

A bright yellow female Centruroides hentzi.

season. These shortened daylight periods may also act as rest times for the body. Apparently, environmental changes should be coordinated with regulated feeding regimens. These regimens should include heavy feeding during warmer times and either lessening or depriving the scorpions of food during cooler times.

Stress

As we have seen, scorpions have excellent sensing abilities and are extremely susceptible to outside influences. To use human terms, they are nervous and high strung. Behavioral biologists call it stress. However, unlike humans where stress is complicated with psychological factors, such as emotions, stress in arachnids is an innate basic physical response to physical stimuli. Scorpions are very simple forms of life, maintaining a highly preconditioned lifestyle. Almost anything out of the ordinary will induce some form of stress, which may cause

abnormal behavioral patterns that are detrimental to their health. The keeper must be constantly aware to avoid situations that will stress their scorpions.

The most obvious reaction to stress is the defensive posture assumed when confronted. The immediate reactions to being uncovered or exposed to light—digging, fleeing, and defensive positioning—are additional, easily noticeable negative responses. Some remain motionless or turn slowly, as if to say, "Hey, who turned on the lights?" Others react by refusing to feed. A few may become aggressive to cage mates, to the point of turning to cannibalism. This is apparent mostly in stressed mother scorpions that suddenly cannibalize their young.

Light Cycles and Vibrations

Two subjects that are rarely considered or discussed are the consequences of day-night light cycles and of ambient vibrations. Both are very important to a scorpion's daily survival.

The elevated straight telson and open chela warn that this **Smerigurus mesaensis** *is at peak arousal and ready to strike.*

However, what about their relationship to seasonal changes and stress?

Light cycles: We know that a scorpion's eyes do little more than see light and dark and most likely inform them that it is time to begin nocturnal activities. Some arachnologists suggest that scorpions can see stars and employ celestial navigation to move about. Research has shown that many lower and higher forms of animal life have varying degrees of this ability. Also, the relationship between seeing and the daily physical and behavioral activities are inborn, controlled mostly by the body's circadian rhythm (biological clock). The eyes also seem to be implicated in reproduction.

Vibrations offer a completely different view on keeping scorpions in captivity. Air and ground sensations are obviously extremely important to the scorpion's daily activities. Not the least of these is stress caused by unfamiliar, abnormal vibrations.

Humans interpret music as stimulating, soothing, and exciting. We can control the quality and loudness to our preferences. Music and voices from radios and televisions reverberate throughout our homes almost constantly. No doubt, a scorpion's sensors also pick up these sounds. After all, music is nothing more than a wide variety of vibrations. How does music affect scorpions? It surely cannot be soothing!

What about footsteps and the plethora of other sounds that we produce but manage to tune out? Practically none of the vibrations of a human's world are commonly encountered in nature. Sit quietly, and absorb the daily racket that constantly inundates our senses. When you isolate and focus on the variety of sounds, you will find them incredibly stressful. Then think of the possible effect this constant noise has on scorpions. I offer no answers, merely thoughts to ponder.

Subtle Annoyances

Many reactions are subtle, so much so that they may be overlooked. Usually they are related to environmental circumstances. A scorpion that climbs and sits atop cage furnishings may be indicating that the substrate is too wet. A scorpion that spends an inordinate amount of time in the water dish may mean that the environment is too dry. A scorpion prowling the cage, particularly during daylight hours, is signaling that something is not right.

The problem may be as straightforward as the scorpion being hungry. However, the scorpion may instead be uncomfortable in its surroundings. This discomfort could be caused by a variety of things: substrate too wet or dry, environment too hot or cold, substrate wrong or dirty, hiding places inadequate, or need for a place to molt. The movement of uneaten and unwanted live prey can be a tactile or sensory annoyance. A worst-case scenario that frequently remains undetected is that the scorpion is infested with mites.

Parasites

Mites are diminutive, almost microscopic parasites that attach themselves to the intersegmental membranes and feed on the scorpion's tissues. They are nocturnal and are seen as tan or white specks on the scorpion. If the infestation is seriously out of control, hundreds may become dislodged from the scorpion and found slowly crawling around the cage or drowned in the water dish. A magnifying glass discloses their eight legs, making identification positive. They are arachnids and belong to the large and diverse order Acarina (20,000 described species) that includes ticks. Several varieties of mites affect scorpions, and they may be host specific. Under normal conditions, scorpions can tolerate a few mites, but heavy infestations can be bothersome or highly stressful.

Mites can be mechanically removed with small forceps or suffocated with a very small drop of either glycerin or fingernail polish. Great care must be taken to avoid getting the substance into the scorpion's chelicerae and spiracles. Remove and isolate the scorpion in a small cage with paper towels. Any loose mites will be easily seen. Changing the paper daily and carefully removing mites from the exoskeleton will likely take a few days.

Discard the substrate, and thoroughly wash the cage with diluted chlorine bleach. A 10 percent solution is perfect. If not disposed of, the furnishings can be soaked in the chlorine solution. Soaps, liquid cleaners (including window cleaners), and disinfectants should not be used, because they may leave harmful residues. Be certain to rinse everything completely with copious amounts of water to remove any chemical residue. When dry, add new substrate, cage furnishings, and the de-mited scorpion.

Mites enter a collection by being carried on food animals, particularly crickets and roaches. They reproduce in moist substrate, not on the scorpions. The eggs hatch, find a host (the scorpion), feed, drop off, and breed, continuing the cycle. Eventually, hundreds of thousands of mites may be produced. If left unchecked, they will probably infest your entire scorpion collection. Warm, damp cages with dead and decaying cricket carcasses are the ultimate breeding grounds. Good housekeeping is an excellent preventive.

The eggs of some mites are found in dry grains and grain products. Aside from their unsightly infestations, they seem to do no harm to scorpions.

Microwaving all grains before using them as food for prey animals and keeping the grains dry will go a long way in preventing the possibility of an epidemic.

Predatory mites: Keepers with large collections of arachnids use a biological control to eliminate parasitic mites. Predatory mites (*Hypoaspis miles*) are released into infected cages, where they seek out and eat the parasitic mites. A few scientific supply companies and arachnid dealers, mostly those dealing in tarantulas, are the best sources. They are used in agriculture to control spider mites on plants. Predatory mites do not seem to bother scorpions or tarantulas but do a great job of exterminating their vexatious relatives.

Internal Parasites

Wild-caught scorpions carry a variety of internal parasites. These normally cause no harm until the animal undergoes severe stress. As has been seen in other animals brought into captivity, particularly amphibians and reptiles, internal parasites can be a serious, debilitating health hazard. Since so little is known about scorpion parasitology and nothing is known about their medical treatment, death is commonly inevitable when the delicate balance is upset. The best preventive is to avoid stressing them.

Internal parasites are mostly acquired from wild food animals and are not often passed on from mothers to offspring. Scorpiophiles hope that nearly every desirable scorpion species will be available from captive breeding. If this occurs, many natural parasites will be lost in these captive animals. This loss has occurred in many different kinds of animals that have been established and bred in captivity for several generations.

Mold

Scorpions may be susceptible to mold. Many mold species are little more than unsightly. However, some appear to interfere with a scorpion's spiracles and book lungs, creating breathing difficulties. Mold affixed to intersegmental membranes may affect movement and cause molting difficulties. Little is known about the adverse effects of mold, but the elimination of molds is an excellent precaution.

Most mold spores are carried in substrate, where they remain dormant until the temperature and humidity conditions are right, enabling them to germinate into mold. A good preventive is to microwave substrate before it is used. Mixing one part sphagnum moss with three parts of the substrate of choice will alter the pH toward the acid side, which frequently prevents many molds from germinating. Sprays and other chemicals should never be used.

Cleanliness Deters Problems

A clean cage is the most effective way of avoiding problems that can endanger or stress your scorpion. When used, be sure water dishes are changed frequently and the gravel is clean. Practice good housekeeping, remove uneaten food and other messes regularly. Do not overdo the cleanliness, though. Arachnids settle down and become familiar with their surroundings. Not only do they remember where things are located, but they also appear to leave chemical or tactile trails in their immediate vicinity. A complete cleaning and replacement of the substrate should be done every six months or more often if needed.

Growth and Molting

As a scorpion grows, its hard exoskeleton becomes too small to contain the larger internal structures. The body forms a new, bigger exoskeleton to replace the too-small one. The process seems simple enough but is actually extremely complex.

Basically, a new outer exoskeleton forms beneath the current one. When it has developed sufficiently, the scorpion goes into hiding, some remaining motionless for as long as a day. Blood (hemolymph) pressure is increased, causing the old exoskeleton to crack along the side and at the front of the prosoma. During the next half day, the appendages are pulled from the old skin in a series of rapid movements followed by periods of rest. All external parts, including the setae, are replaced by a molt. The shed is a translucent replica of the scorpion and retains the ability to fluoresce under UV light.

Shedding is a tenuous time for a scorpion. If it is disturbed or the moisture is not quite right, the old exoskeleton may adhere to the new one. If they bind together, the exoskeletons cannot be separated. The luckless scorpion will die.

The newly emergent scorpion is white, extremely soft bodied, and extremely vulnerable at this time. They do not fluoresce in this state. As the new exoskeleton hardens, it darkens. The

This 3rd instar **Vaejovis spinigerus,** *nearly free from its molted exoskeleton, is vulnerable until its chitinous outer surface can harden.*

ability to fluoresce returns. The fluorescent material is found in only one layer of the cured exoskeleton.

Other than increased size, no structures are added or deleted during all the molts except the first and last ones. Actually, that is not totally true; appendages that have been broken off might partially regenerate. Little has been reported about the extent of regeneration in scorpions. However, total regeneration of parts is common in some other arachnids, particularly spiders.

Changes at the First and Last Molts

Important physical changes occur with the first molt into the second instar. These include formation of most setae, surface granulation,

the daily physical abuse and abrasion to the exoskeleton would wear it thin over time. This is another concept that needs to be investigated.

Depending on the species, scorpions molt five to nine times before reaching maturity. A scorpion may take from six months to more than seven years to attain adulthood. The length of time varies among different taxa. Smaller species mature rapidly, reproduce earlier, gestate for briefer periods, and have shorter life spans. Larger taxa (such as *Pandinus* and *Heterometrus*) can reach sexual maturity within 10–14 months. However, other genera (such as, *Hadogenes*) may take two or more years.

Preventing Injuries

Communally kept scorpions periodically undergo territorial skirmishes and fights. Sometimes these get a bit rough, and an appendage may be damaged or torn off. There is always the possibility of fatal envenomation and/or cannibalism occurring. The latter is a particular threat to a scorpion that has just molted. During the typical seven to ten days for the exoskeleton to harden following a molt, the scorpion is very susceptible to predation or injury. These are the chances taken in communal situations. Having a cage large enough to accommodate the animals adequately, providing plenty of hiding places, and being certain they are well fed will all help prevent difficulties.

Cage furnishings used as retreats should be placed or stacked in a way that they will not fall and crush the captive. This is particularly

teeth on the cutting edges of the chelae and chelicerae, and hardening of the chelicerae, chelae, and telson. Secondary sexual characters are prominently differentiated in the last molt. No one is certain if scorpions molt after they have reached adulthood. Several researchers have reported that males, at least, do not. Wild-caught adult scorpions frequently have worn chelicerae and tarsal structures, supporting the hypothesis that they do not molt after maturing. It seems that females of long-lived taxa would have to molt again. Because they may live 15 years or longer beyond the adult molt, important with scorpions that dig a lot. Pieces of lightweight cork bark curls make excellent retreats. Remember that scorpions like to be in contact with the walls of their tunnels or scrapes, so the cavity should be little more than adequate in size.

Adding a cactus to a desert cage may add aesthetic appeal, but it increases the chance of an injury. Many cacti and succulents have extremely sharp spines that could pierce the softer parts of a scorpion's body. I suggest you use plastic substitutes if you feel you must decorate your cages.

Falls: Even though the exoskeleton is hard, it is not a foolproof protection. The exoskeleton is highly susceptible to cracking if impacted. Potentially, the most menacing cause of this type of injury is a fall. It is unlikely that such a fall will happen in a cage since the height is rarely enough to permit a serious drop. Damaging falls usually occur during transporting, cage cleaning, and handling. Many things easily frighten scorpions, and they quickly react by running away. Moving them is extremely disorienting and stressful.

Whenever a scorpion is taken from its cage, it should be enclosed in a covered container. Few things are more tragic and frustrating for a keeper than watching a scorpion lying on the floor, twitching as body fluids ooze from a split in its mesosomal membrane. In all but a very few cases, nothing can be done to close the wound and save the animal. It is best destroyed to stop its suffering.

Wound care: Applying something to cover, clot, or gel leaking hemolymph may close a small wound, but a large one will probably cause the scorpion to "bleed" to death. In the wild, incidental injuries are sealed when particles of sand or soil adhere to the hemolymph, effectively sealing the wound. In captivity, talcum powder or a dab of nail polish have been effective in some instances. A variety of products known as liquid skin, sold in pharmacies for closing small cuts to human skin, also work. Taking great care to avoid and prevent an accident is the only proven cure.

Proper Humidity

Because it is commonly overlooked and causes the deaths of thousands of captive scorpions annually, one idea has been repeated throughout this book—the scorpion's need for moisture. Water is a necessary part of all living cells and must be renewed periodically. Scorpions are known to drink water, but most of it is taken from the food they eat. Aside from these sources, at the very least, some moisture appears to be necessary for scorpions to survive.

Scorpions from tropical rain forests rely heavily on external sources, while those from extremely arid areas may accept it opportunistically. First instars will usually desiccate if they are deprived of moisture provided from contact with their mother. It is conjectured that advance instars and adults cannot absorb moisture from their environment through their waxy, hardened exoskeletons. This may or may not be true. Some water may be passed through the intersegmental membranes. Water is lost through the unhardened skin of newly molted scorpions. It is highly likely that absorption is possible at that time as well.

Desert species frequently live in burrows or under rocks and ground debris—places that maintain some moisture. Scorpion burrows are reported to retain relative humidity, as high as

50–70 percent. This may provide cooling by evaporation and be important to the molting process. Numerous species remain dormant during the driest months, coming to the surface with the advent of rains. In many desert regions, morning dew forms on rocks, plants, and other objects (including the exposed bodies of some animals). This dew is regularly drunk by lizards, insects, and other small animals. There is no reason that scorpions would not do likewise.

One way to avoid the potential desiccation problem partially is to provide a shallow dish of water for all scorpions periodically. Those requiring high humidity (such as tropical rain forest scorpions) should have water at all times, and their cages should be lightly misted at least every few days. The substrate should never be allowed to dry out completely.

Scorpions from unknown microhabitats should have water available periodically and be tested (as suggested in the section on cage furnishings) to determine their needs. Subadult and small forms from all but the most arid environments can desiccate rapidly, so their water supplies should be monitored often. Many more scorpions die from desiccation than starvation. The keeper should therefore make fresh water available periodically.

A Few Final Thoughts

Because scientific grants are becoming extremely difficult to obtain, the emphasis of most research has been placed on finding data that directly benefit humans. Corporations, institutions, and government and private agencies often show little if any interest in funding natural history studies. This has enabled the investigations and observations of dedicated

and astute individuals to become a primary instrument and conduit for unlocking many of nature's mysteries.

If you go into the field and collect scorpions, please take the utmost care to replace objects you turn. Always be aware that you are impacting the environment. By respecting our natural world, you are looking to the future. We are all aware that many habitats are in a precarious state, but too few realize the serious consequences that our mere presence places on microhabitats. Every attempt should be made to leave everything as close as possible to how you found it. Take only the animals that you can properly care for.

Very little time and energy is needed for you to make a contribution to the science of arachnology. By keeping accurate notes of exactly where the animal was captured and the conditions at the site, the animal has continuing value even after it has died. Preserving scorpions is easy. Simply submerse the dead animal in a small container of rubbing (isopropyl) alcohol, and include a label written in pencil with its collecting data. The information must be accurate. The best specimens are those that have recently died and not had time to decompose.

Contact a local natural history museum or college biology department, and tell them what you have. Known as voucher specimens, these preserved animals provide an accurate identification and locality for someone studying scorpion fauna. It is possible that the animal has not been reported from the area. Who knows, it might be an undescribed species. A great deal of information has been furnished by careful, dedicated, amateur arachnologists.

As we have seen in this small book, keeping scorpions offers numerous challenges and the

This extreme low angle shows the formidable readiness of this foraging **Opistophthalmus boehmi.**

opportunity for discovery. Your findings, as insignificant as they may seem to you, are an important addition to understanding the complexity of our rapidly diminishing natural world.

The role of feeding, temperature, humidity, and seasonal changes in the natural history of scorpions is just beginning to be understood. However, there is an important lesson to be learned from the hobby of herpetoculture. "Pushing" amphibians and reptiles to reach adulthood and reproduce has caused many of

the problems associated with their captive breeding. Arachnoculturists must not fall into this trap. As keepers, we should help the natural progression of a scorpion by supporting the animal's needs, not dictating and changing them for our own whims or gain.

Scorpions have been a successful, viable part of the natural world for hundreds of millions of years. Their ability to adapt and survive cannot be taken lightly. They must be doing something right!

Antivenin (Antivenom) Support in the United States

Arizona Poison Control Center
1-800-222-1222 (available 24 hours)
www.pharmacy.arizona.edu/outreach/poison/

Miami-Dade Fire Rescue (Antivenin Bank)
1-786-336-6600 (available 24 hours)
www.miami-dadefirerescue.com/

Arthropod Societies

These organizations publish journals, newsletters, and/or arachnid-related materials. Membership is highly recommended to serious scorpion enthusiasts. Dues are required for most.

American Tarantula Society
www.asthq.org

American Arachnological Society
www.americanarachnology.org/

British Tarantula Society
www.thebts.co.uk/

Euscopius
www.science.marshall.edu/fet/euscorpius/pubs. htm

Sonoran Arthropod Studies Institute
www.sasionline.org/

Internet Sites

Logging on to any of the following web sites will link to a myriad of other related sites. Unfortunately, many of these other sites are short-lived, beginning and ending almost spontaneously. All offer an excellent method of communicating with other arachnophiles throughout the world. They are the best way to ask questions and exchange pertinent, timely information that is frequently unavailable anywhere else.

Arachnoboards
www.arachnoboards.com/ab/

Arachnodata Home Page
www.arachnodata.ch/

Emperor Scorpion Home Page
http://home.mindspring.com/~drrod1/

Kari's Scorpion Pages
www.angelfire.com/tx4/scorpiones/index.html

Operation Scorpion
http//library.thinkquest.org/27858/map.htm

Pet Bugs.com
www.petbugs.com/

Singapore Scorpion Page
http://members.tripod.com/~c_kianwee/ welcome.html

South African Scorpions
www.scorpions.co.za.htm

The Scorpion Files
www.ub.ntnu.no/scorpion-files/

Scorpion Ring
www.angelfire.com/ks2/scorplinkpage/

The Spiral Burrow
www.thedailylink.com/thespiralburrow/index. html

The Venom List: For All Things Venomous
www.venomlist.com

Scorpion Sources

Many local pet stores (particularly those specializing in amphibians and reptiles) carry scorpions and are therefore logical places to buy your first one. Scorpions are frequently available at reptile shows that are held periodically in various parts of the country. Additional sources will be found at the Internet sites listed above.

Crickets, Mealworms, Fruit Flies, and Other Food Animals and Supplies

There are many food animal suppliers throughout the United States. Check your local telephone book under "Bait" for one nearest to you.

The only scorpion known in Hawaii, Southeast Asian native Isometrus maculatus *has managed to stow away and be carried to ports throughout the world, establishing viable colonies far from its point of origin.*

Suggested Reading

The following publications are excellent sources of information about scorpions and are in print or available at major libraries.

Brodie, E. D., and J. D. Dawson, *Venomous Animals. Golden Guide*, Golden Books Publishing Company, New York, NY. 2000.

Dunn, G. A., *The Insect Study Sourcebook: An International Entomology Resource Guide*, Special Publication #1, 5th edition, Young Entomologist's Society, Lansing, MI. 1994.

Fet, V., W. D. Sissom, G. Lowe, and M. E. Braunwalter, *Catalog of the Scorpions of the World (1958–1998)*, Entomological Society of New York, NY. 2000.

Gaban, R. D., *Gaban's Scorpion Tales*, American Tarantula Society, Carlsbad, NM.1998.

Keegan, H. L., *Scorpions of Medical Importance*, University of Mississippi, New York, NY. 1980.

Levi, H. W., and L. R. Levi, *Spiders and Their Kin. A Golden Guide*, Golden Press, New York, NY. 1990.

Levy, G., and P. Amitai, *Scorpiones. Fauna Palaestina. Arachnida I*, Israel Academy of Sciences and Humanities, Jerusalem. 1980.

Marshall, S. D., *Tarantulas and Other Arachnids*, Barron's Educational Series, Inc., Hauppauge, NY. 1996.

Polis, G., ed., *Biology of Scorpions*. Stanford University Press, Stanford, CA. 1990.

Young Entomologist's Society, Inc., *Caring for Insect Livestock: An Insect Rearing Manual. Special Publication #8*, Young Entomologist's Society, Lansing, MI. 1993.

Table of Captive Conditions

The scorpions listed in this table are taxa frequently available in the pet trade. Not all are addressed in the text. However, the characteristics shown in these tables should enable proper care to be given to them. Be aware that many scorpions look alike, and dealers frequently misidentify them.

Arachnologists have suggested that some of the species included here should be reassigned to different families. Scorpion taxonomy is dynamic, and the results of current research have produced conflicting views. Until more data is available to reach a consensus, the assignments used in this book will suffice. For simplicity, the species are presented alphabetically by family and follow the *Catalog of the Scorpions of the World (1758–1998)* (see "Scorpion Taxonomy," page 19).

Scorpions with either four or five skulls and crossbones (☠☠☠☠ or ☠☠☠☠☠) are taxa considered to be extremely venomous, life-threatening species. The toxicity may vary among specimens of the same species. These scorpions are included here so their husbandry data are available to keepers requiring it. Experienced keepers should give extensive thought before deciding to keep any of the species, and then do so with full knowledge of the danger and possible implications these scorpions carry. **Under NO circumstances should a novice attempt to keep any of these scorpions.**

Scorpions with either two or three skulls and crossbones (☠☠ or ☠☠☠) are also dangerous and cause serious envenomations. Their venom will most likely not kill adult humans but will cause extremely painful repercussions. Older adults,

adults with weakened immune systems, and children are at greater risk for serious repercussions.

Scorpions with one skull and crossbones (☠) are considered to be harmless or moderately venomous. They are very good scorpions for the novice keeper. Envenomation will cause discomfort and pain on a par with a bee sting.

Remember: All scorpion stings (envenomations) cause reactions. Some people have much more severe reactions and complications than others. The best preventative is not to be stung.

Legend

Venom		Habitat		Substrate	
🦂	= Very mild venom	A	= Arid	R	= Rock (flat), ceramic tile
🦂🦂	= Mild venom	G	= Grassland/savanna/ temperate	S	= Soil (potting mix)
🦂🦂🦂	= Moderate venom			ls	= Loose sand
🦂🦂🦂🦂	= Dangerous (serious medical implications)	F	= Forest	sc	= Scrape
		T	= Tropical	vb	= Vertical bark
		D	= Cave and environs	H	= Heavy
		B	= Bark	L	= Light or lightly
🦂🦂🦂🦂🦂	= Very dangerous (has caused human fatalities)	C	= Composite sand/tamped	M	= Moderate or moderately
		P	= Peat, mulch, coconut husk	N	= No or never
				O	= Occasionally

A Quick Reference of Various Scorpion Species

	Family	Toxicity	Habitat	Substrate	Burrower	Climber
Androctonus amoreuxi	Buthidae	🦂🦂🦂🦂+	A	CR	sc	Y
Androctonus australis	Buthidae	🦂🦂🦂🦂🦂	A	CR	sc	Y
Androctonus bicolor	Buthidae	🦂🦂🦂🦂+	A	CR	sc	Y
Androctonus crassicauda	Buthidae	🦂🦂🦂🦂🦂	A	CR	Osc	Y
Androctonus mauritanicus	Buthidae	🦂🦂🦂🦂+	A	CR	sc	Y
Babycurus jacksoni	Buthidae	🦂🦂🦂	GFT	PS	sc	Y
Bothriurus bonariensis	Bothriuridae	🦂	G	Cls	Ysc	N
Brachistosternus ehrenbergi	Bothriuridae	🦂	A	Cls	Ysc	N
*Buthus occitanus (1)**	Buthidae	🦂🦂	AG	SCR	Y	N
*Buthus occitanus (2)**	Buthidae	🦂🦂🦂+	AG	lsR	Y	N
Centruroides exilicauda	Buthidae	🦂🦂🦂	AG	CRB	scB	Y
Centruroides gracilis	Buthidae	🦂🦂🦂	GFT	SPB	scB	Y
Centruroides guanensis	Buthidae	🦂+	GFT	CRB	scB	Y
Centruroides hentzi	Buthidae	🦂🦂	GFT	CRB	scB	Y
Centruroides margaritatus	Buthidae	🦂🦂+	GFT	PSB	scB	Y
Centruroides vittatus	Buthidae	🦂🦂+	AG	CRB	scB	Y
Chaerilus celebensis	Chaerilidae	🦂	FT	CPS	Ysc	N
Diplocentrus lindo	Diplocentridae	🦂	AGF	CRS	Ysc	N
Diplocentrus peloncillensis	Diplocentridae	🦂	GF	CRS	Ysc	N
Diplocentrus spitzeri	Diplocentridae	🦂	G	CRS	scR	N
Euscorpius italicus	Euscorpiidae	🦂	GF	CPS	R	N
Hadruroides charcasus	Iuridae	🦂🦂	A	CSR	O	N
Hadrurus arizonensis	Iuridae	🦂🦂	A	CRB	C	N
Hadrurus spadix	Iuridae	🦂🦂	A	CRB	C	N
Hadogenes paucidens	Liochelidae	🦂	AGF	CR	R	Y
Hadogenes troglodytes	Liochelidae	🦂	AGF	CR	R	Y
Heterometrus cyaneus	Scorpionidae	🦂	FT	PSB	Y	N

Q	= Quick	⇓	= Low humidity (less than 50%)	?	= Not sure or may vary
V	= Very	⇑	= High humidity (greater than 70%)	1×	= Once a week
Y	= Yes	⇒	= Moderate humidity (50%–70%)	1-2	= Once or twice a week
vs	= 1 ⇓ in. (2.5 ⇓ cm)	±	= More or less	4±	= Monthly (more or less)
s	= 1-2.5 in. (2.5–6.4 cm)	–	= To, between	W	= Weekly
m	= 2.5-3.5 in. (6.4-8.9 cm)	+	= More	↓	= Winter cool period suggested (10–15°F/ 5–8°C lower)
l	= 3.5-4.5 ⇑ in. (8.9-11.4 ⇑ cm)	–	= Less		
vl	= 4.5-5.5 in. (11.4-14.0 cm)				
xl	= 5.5 ⇑ in. (14.0 ⇑ cm)				

Vertical Hide	Defensive	Speed	Canabilistic	Size	Optimal Temp F° (Daytime)	Optimal Temp C° (Daytime)	Humidity	Mist Frequency	Water Dish
N	V	Q	Y	l-vl	85±	29.4±	⇓	4±	0
N	V	Q	Y	l-vl	85±	29.4±	⇓	4±	0
N	V	Q	Y	m-l	85±	29.4±	⇓	4±	0
N	V	Q	Y	m-l	85±	29.4±	⇓	4±	0
N	V	Q	Y	m-l	85±	29.4±	⇓	4±	0
Y	V	Q	N	s	80±	26.7±	⇒	1-2	Y
N	N	M	N	m	70±	21.1±	⇓	N	4±
N	?	?	?	m	70±	21.±	⇓	N	4±
N	Y	Q	Y	s-m	85±	26.7±	⇒	0	W
N	Y	Q	Y	s-m	85±	29.4±	⇓	N	Y
Y	M	Q	N	s-m	85±	26.7±	⇓	0	4±
Y	M	Q	N	s-m	75+	23.9+	⇒	W	4±Y
Y	M	Q	N	vs	80±	26.7±	⇒	W	W
Y	M	Q	N	vs	80±	26.7±	⇒	W	W
Y	Y	Q	N	s-m	80±	29.4±	⇒	W	W
Y	M	Q	N	m	85±	26.7±	⇒	0	W
N	N	M	N	s	80±	26.7±	⇑	1-2	Y
N	M	M	M	s-m	80±	26.7±	⇒	W	Y
N	M	M	M	s-m	80±	26.7±	⇒	W	Y
N	M	M	M	s-m	80±	26.7±	⇒	W	Y
N	M	M	Y	s	75±	23.9±	⇒	W	Y
N	M	Q		m	80±	26.7±	⇓	?	W
N	Y	Q	Y	l-vl	85±	29.4±	⇓	0	W
N	Y	Q	Y	l-vl	85±	29.4±	⇓	0	W
Y	Y	M	0	l-xl	80±	26.7±	⇒-	N	4±
Y	Y	M	0	l-xl	80±	26.7±	⇒-	N	4±
N	M	M	N	l-vl	85±	29.4±	⇑	1-2	Y

	Family	Toxicity	Habitat	Substrate	Burrower	Climber
Heterometrus fulvipes	Scorpionidae	☠	FT	PSB	Y	N
Heterometrus longimanus	Scorpionidae	☠	FT	PSB	Y	O
Heterometrus spinifer	Scorpionidae	☠	FT	PSB	Y	O
Hottentotta caboverdensis	Buthidae	☠☠☠	AG	CSR	O	N
Hottentotta judaicus	Buthidae	☠☠☠	AG	CRB	sc	N
Hottentotta trilineatus	Buthidae	☠☠☠	AG	CRB	sc	N
Iomachus politus	Liochelidae	☠	GFT	PSB	B	N
Isometrus maculatus	Buthidae	☠☠	GT	SB	B	Y
Leiurus quinquestriatus	Buthidae	☠☠☠☠☠	A	CR	Y	O
Liocheles australasiae	Liochelidae	☠	GFT	PSB	B	O
Lychas mucronatus	Buthidae	☠☠☠	GFT	PSB	SB	Y
Mesobuthus martensii	Buthidae	☠☠☠	G	CR	Y	N
Odonturus dentatus	Buthidae	☠☠☠	GFT	PS	scB	N
Opistacanthus asper	Liochelidae	☠	AGF	CSB	N	Y
Opistophthalmus boemi	Scorpionidae	☠☠	G	AGF	Y	N
Opistophthalmus ecristatus	Scorpionidae	☠☠	G	AGF	Y	N
Opistophthalmus glabrifrons	Scorpionidae	☠☠	AG	CPS	Y	N
Opistophthalmus wahlbergii	Scorpionidae	☠☠	AG	CPS	Y	N
Orthochirus scrobiculosus	Buthidae	☠☠☠	AG	CRS	scR	N
Pandinus cavimanus	Scorpionidae	☠	FT	PSB	Y	N
Pandinus imperator	Scorpionidae	☠	FT	PSB	Y	N
Parabuthus liosoma	Buthidae	☠☠☠	AG	CRB	Ysc	O
Parabuthus mossambicensis	Buthidae	☠☠☠+	AG	CRB	Ysc	N
Parabuthus transvaalicus	Buthidae	☠☠☠☠+	AG	CRB	Ysc	N
Paruroctonus boreus	Vaejovidae	☠	AG	CPS	RB	N
Pseudouroctonus reddelli	Vaejovidae	☠	DR	CR	Y	N
Rhopalurus junceus	Buthidae	☠☠☠	GFT	CSB	scR	O
Scorpio maurus palmatus	Scorpionidae	☠☠	AG	CPS	Y	O
Smeringurus mesaensis	Vaejovidae	☠☠	A	IsR	Y	N
Tityus bahiensis	Buthidae	☠☠☠☠+	GFT	PSB	Ysc	Y
Tityus falconensis	Buthidae	☠☠☠☠	GFT	PSB	Ysc	Y
T. stigmurus var. confluenciata	Buthidae	☠☠☠☠+	GFT	CPS	Ysc	Y
Tityus stigmurus	Buthidae	☠☠☠☠	GFT	PSB	Ysc	Y
Tityus trinitatis	Buthidae	☠☠☠☠	GFT	PSB	Ysc	Y
Uroctonus mordax	Vaejovidae	☠	GF	BPS	Ysc	N
Vaejovis carolinianus	Vaejovidae	☠	GF	BPS	scB	O
Vaejovis coahuilae	Vaejovidae	☠☠	AGF	CB	Y	N
Vaejovis confusus	Vaejovidae	☠☠	AG	BPS	scR	N
Vaejovis spinigerus	Vaejovidae	☠☠	AG	BPS	scR	N

(1) darker-colored European species complex (several newly described species); (2) yellow-colored North African species complex (several newly described species).

Vertical Hide	Defensive	Speed	Canabilistic	Size	Optimal Temp F° (Daytime)	Optimal Temp C° (Daytime)	Humidity	Mist Frequency	Water Dish
N	M	M	N	l–vl	85±	29.4±	⇑	1–2	Y
Y	M	M	N	l–xl	85±	29.4±	⇑	1–2	Y
Y	M	M	N	l–vl	85±	29.4±	⇑	1–2	Y
N	Y	Q	N	M	85±	29.4±	⇒	0	0
N	Y	Q	Y	m	85±	29.4±	⇓	W	0
N	Y	Q	N	m	85±	29.4±	⇓	W	0
N	N	M	N	s–m	80±	26.7±	⇑	W	Y
Y	Y	Q	N	s–m	80–	26.7–	⇒	1–2	Y
N	V	Q	Y	m–l	85+	29.4±	⇓	4±	0
Y	N	Q	N	s	80±	26.7±	⇑	1–2	Y
Y	Y	Q	N	vs	80±	26.7±	⇒	1–2	Y
N	M	Q	N	s–m	80±	26.7±	⇒	0	0
N	Y	Q	N	m	80±	26.7±	⇒	W	Y
N	Y	M	N	s–m	80±	26.7±	⇒–	W	Y
N	0	Q	Y	m	85±	29.4±	⇒	0	W
N	0	Q	Y	m–l	85±	29.4±	⇒	0	W
N	Y	Q	Y	m–l	85±	29.4±	⇒	0	W
N	Y	Q	Y	m–l	85±	29.4±	⇒	0	W
N	N	M	N	s	85±	29.4±	⇓	4±	0
N	M	M	N	l–vl	85±	29.4±	⇑V	1–2	Y
N	M	M	N	l–xl	85±	29.4±	V⇑	1–2	Y
N	M	Q	Y	m–l	80±	26.7±	⇓	0	W
N	Y	Q	Y	m–l	80±	26.7±	⇓	0	W
N	V	M	Y	l–xl	85±	29.4±	⇓	0	W
N	M	M	Y	s–m	80±	26.7±	⇒	1–2	W
N	V	V	Y	m	85±	29.4±	V	N	4±
Y	M	Q	N	m	80–	26.7–	⇒	W	W
Y	Y	Q	Y	m	75+	23.9+	⇒+	W	W
N	V	V	Y	l–vl	85±	29.4±	V	N	4±
Y	M	Q	N	s	80±	26.7±	⇒	W	W
Y	M	Q	N	s	80±	26.7±	⇒	W	W
Y	V	Q	N	s	80±	26.7±	⇑	W	W
Y	M	Q	N	s	80±	26.7±	⇒	W	W
Y	M	Q	N	s	80±	26.7±	⇒	W	W
N	Y	M	N	m	75±	23.9±	⇑	1×	W
Y	V	V	N	s	80±	26.7±	⇒	4±	Y
N	V	V	N	s	85±	29.4±	⇓	N	4±
N	V	V	N	s	85±	29.4±	⇓	N	4±
N	V	V	N	m	85±	29.4±	⇓	N	4±

About the Author

Manny Rubio is a commercial photographer, author, and naturalist who has photographed wildlife throughout the world. His photographs have been widely published, and he has more than 500 magazine covers to his credit. He has written more than 100 articles, mostly on herpetology and arachnids. In 1999, Smithsonian Press published his highly acclaimed book on rattlesnakes.

Acknowledgments

This updated edition would not have been accomplished without the prompting and promoting of Barron's editor Mark Miele. I would like to offer special thanks to Kari McWest and Lucian Ross for reviewing the manuscript and offering their much-needed comments and suggestions. Thanks to Jan Ove Rein (Norway) and Eric Yither (France) for their input and help with revamping and expanding the captive-condition tables. I have unfailing gratitude to my wife Beth for putting up with an ever-fluctuating number of cages of scorpions. Finally, I would be remiss if I did not acknowledge the dozens of scorpion cyber buddies worldwide who unselfishly pass along their observations, findings, and (occasionally) scorpions with the hope of furthering the hobby of scorpion keeping.

Important Note

Scorpion venom is potentially dangerous, and some may be life threatening. Stings should never be taken lightly, particularly if the animal is known to have a highly toxic venom, or the keeper has been previously stung or is prone to allergic reactions.

The author and publisher recommend that scorpions should not be handled at any time. Anyone keeping scorpions must understand the potential danger to themselves and others, and take extreme measures to prevent a sting or an animal's escape. Check your state regulations to assure that you can legally keep scorpions, and to see if a permit is required.

Photo Credits

All photos, including covers, by Manny Rubio.

Uncredited Species

From front cover: *Centruroides gracilis*; inside front cover: *Heterometrus fulvipes*; pp. 2–3: *Smerigurus mesaensis*; p. 5: *Liocheles australasiae*; p. 11: *Diplocentrus spitzeri*; p. 15: *Pseudouroctonus apacheanus*; p. 19: *Centruroides gracilis*; p. 27: *Heterometrus longimanus*; p. 33: *Heterometrus cyaneus*; p. 77; *Hadrurus spadix*; p. 87: *Tityus stigmurus*; p. 95: *Liocheles waigiensis*; p. 107: *Androctonus australis;* inside back cover: *Isometrus maculatus*; back cover: *Heterometrus spinifer*.

All inquiries should be addressed to:
Barron's Educational Series, Inc.
250 Wireless Boulevard
Hauppauge, NY 11788
www.barronseduc.com

ISBN-13: 978-0-7641-3981-9
ISBN-10: 0-7641-3981-9

Library of Congress Catalog Card No. 2007028727

Library of Congress Cataloging-in-Publication Data
Rubio, Manny.
    Scorpions : everything about purchase, care, feeding, behavior, and breedubg / Manny Rubio.
        p. cm.
    Includes index.
    ISBN-13: 978-0-7641-3981-9 (alk. paper)
    ISBN-10: 0-7641-3981-9 (alk. paper)
        1. Scorpions as pets. I. Title.

SF459.S35R83   2008
639'.7–dc22   2007028727

Printed in China
9 8 7 6 5 4 3 2 1